W9-CCD-126

PRAYING THE BOOK
OF JOB

PRAYING THE BOOK

OF JOB

To Understand Trouble and Suffering

By
Elmer Towns

CONTENTS

READING HELPS

THE Book of Job was the first book written in the Bible. It represents the thoughts and logic of the early patriarchs. Even though early and embryonic, it contains the root fundamentals of Christianity. It contains a view of a sovereign God, Creator, guide, and judge of all men. The author tells us salvation is found only in God and even though we pass through the inevitability of death, yet there is coming a resurrection when we shall see God. The righteous will live with God and the wicked will be punished in Sheol (Hell).

The Book of Job is written in Hebrew poetry—not like English with rhyme and meter. The Hebrew writer *compares* the context of the first phrase with the next. Hebrew poetry matches *thoughts*, not rhyme or meter. There are four distinct types of poetry written by the ancients.

1. *Synonymous poetry*: the thought in the first line is repeated in the next line.

> *God moves mountains without asking anyone;*
> *They quake because He speaks.*
> *God shakes the earth according to His will;*
> *The foundations tremble* (Job 9:5-6).

2. *Antithetic poetry*: the thought of the second line is the opposite of the first line.

> *God gives hope to the poor*
> *But He breaks the fangs of the wicked* (Job 5:16).

3. *Synthetic poetry*: the first line begins making a statement and the second or third line completes the thought.

> *Eliphaz told Job to listen to his advice,*

Repent of his sin that caused his trouble and,
Turn to God with all his heart.
Then God would restore his property
And again bless his life (Job 5:27).

4. *Climactic poetry*: the first line is incomplete without a completing thought in the second and third line.

Eliphaz told Job even a fool could turn to God
And have momentary success and prosperity;
Just as Job had temporary wealth but lost it all (Job 5:3).

I believe in the inspiration of every word in the original languages of the Bible and to that I add, I believe in the inerrancy of the thoughts expressed by inspirational words. What you're holding in your hand is not a word-for-word translation from the original Hebrew to modern day English—that would be called a modern Bible translation. The first step is translation, the second step is interpretation, and the third step is application. This book includes all three steps. First, I have translated the Scriptures; second, I have interpreted and applied them in what you read here. So, as you read this book, compare it to your Bible.

I've written this book to help you understand why there is suffering in the world and what God wants to accomplish through it. Also, I want you to recognize the wrong reactions to suffering. Some of the "poor theology" you might hear in hospitals today is as old as Job.

You might want to read one or two chapters each day for your devotion. Pray as you read each section. Talk to God through the words of this book, then let God talk to you.

PREFACE

God guided me to write this book, but of course I feel that way about every book I write. I began writing about Job's suffering from an intellectual point of view. I studied encyclopedias to understand Job's unique sickness, then I poured over my Thesaurus to find inventive ways to describe his suffering.

But something happened halfway through this project that jerked me into reality—I had a colonoscopy. The doctor said, "You have a tumor the size of an egg." He couldn't bring himself to say the "C" word. Within two weeks, I was in surgery that was supposed to last an hour and a half. Four and a half hours later, I woke up. The doctor said, "The tumor was the size of a grapefruit causing complications; nevertheless, we got it all." No sign of cancer in the surrounding tissue or lymph nodes.

It took 19 staples to close up the incision that seemed two feet long. After the anesthesia wore off, pain wrenched my midsection. I entered the world of Job. "Why this pain?" and "Why cancer?" and "Why me?" It took my wife and a nurse to pull me out of the bed, accompanied with agonizing groans.

When I was a college freshman, my Bible teacher told the class, "You're too young to fully understand Job." He went on to say, "As you grow older, you'll go through disappointments, pain, and black despair...then you'll empathize with Job's suffering." My teacher explained that we freshmen would probably be perplexed by Job's poetry, but later in life we would identify with Job's anguish, then—and only then—could we understand this book.

AMEN. I now add my agreement to that observation.

I don't wish suffering on anyone so you can enter the message of Job. But trials will come as Job observed, *"Man is born to trouble, as the sparks fly upward"* (Job 5:7). So this book will be here for you when they come.

In my darkest hours I re-read some of my early translations as though I had never seen these passages in Job. God spoke to me through my transliterations as though Job were in the next bed talking to me. And the amazing parallel—God helped me through my suffering with my own penmanship.

For those of you who want to know how I wrote this book: First, I translated the passage from Hebrew into English. Then I transliterated the passage into the second person so each verse becomes a prayer to address God. So this is not a translation of Scripture, but a paraphrase so you can apply the message of Job to your life by prayer and meditation.

This book is not just a translation to help you know better the Book of Job, but this is a devotional to help you know God. So reach out to touch God as you pray the Book of Job, but more importantly; let God touch you.

Written from my home
at the foothills of the Blue Ridge Mountains,
Elmer L. Towns
Fall 2005

INTRODUCTION TO THE BOOK OF JOB

THE Book of Job tells the amazing story of a man who held tenaciously to his integrity in the face of pain, loss, darkness, and even death. Job's integrity tells its own story that a man's relationship to God is more important than anything else, even his own physical life.

The Book of Job teaches its own lesson that in this world there is sickness, pain, and loss. Trouble comes to the just and unjust. This story also tells that friends can give the wrong advice to those who are sick. Job's friends had a personal agenda when comforting him and their worst advice was that Job was suffering because he had sinned against God.

During the Old Testament, the Book of Job was placed in the third section of the Jewish canon. It appeared in a section called writings (wisdom books) and was located next to Psalms and Proverbs—near the top of the reading list. However, the book was not designated for public reading in the synagogues. Rather, it was for private reading, especially for the more thoughtful believers in God.

Look at the Book of Job carefully; it is a people's book. It doesn't mention priests, prophets, or any of God's special servants. It doesn't mention the sanctuary, the Tabernacle, or the Temple. It is not a great hymn of praise or a book of passionate pursuits of God. Rather, the Book of Job deals with one of the greatest issues in life: why do bad things happen to good people?

Where Did Job Live?

The Book of Job takes place in the land of Uz, a little-known region miles south of the Dead Sea in the Sinai Peninsula. Uz was named after Huz, the first-born son of Nahor (Gen. 22:21, see original language). And as we shall see later, this placed Job in the Sinai Peninsula about the time Moses was a shepherd there. Also see Appendix A.

Who Was Job?

There was much speculation about the identity of Job. Many believe he was a contemporary of Abraham, a patriarch who led his family in worship of God, and as a patriarch-priest, sacrificed for the sins of his family. Both Job and Abraham did this.

Some liberal scholars place Job living near the time of Babylon captivity, but there is no internal support in the book that places Job near the end of the Old Testament.

However, some Hebrew scholars believe Job was the son of Issachar (Gen. 46:13). Issachar was one of the 12 sons of Jacob who eventually went down to Egypt to live (Gen. 46:3). Since we believe the Bible best interprets itself, we solve the problems of date, identity, and location by looking into Scripture itself. There is no reason to believe that Job is not one of the sons of Issachar.

Issachar was approximately 40 years old when he went down to Egypt. That suggests his third son, Job, (Gen. 46:13) would have been about 20 years old at that time (1706 B.C.). While most of Israel originally prospered in Egypt under Joseph, apparently Job never went to Egypt with his parents. Maybe he returned back to the Sinai Peninsula to live in Uz. It was there Job accumulated his wealth and prosperity.

Job was approximately 70 years old when his wealth and health were taken away (Job 1,2). When he was restored God gave him a "double blessing" (Gen. 42:19), which would imply that he lived another 140 years. Apparently Job was 210 years old when he died.

Authorship of the Book of Job

When Job died (1516 B.C.), Moses was 55 years old and had already spent 15 years in the Sinai Peninsula watching his sheep. I believe Job and Moses not only overlapped each other because they lived in the same area, they probably knew each other. Perhaps Moses was an "ear-witness" of the content of the book as Job told him the stories of losing his wealth and the hypocritical speeches of the three "comforters." Also, perhaps Moses was an "eye witness" of Job's home in Uz, Job's family, and may have even met some of Job's friends. I think Job told his amazing story of suffering to Moses who wrote it down. Moses kept the manuscript; eventually adding it to the collection of the first five books of the Old Testament.

The fact that Job is the son of Issachar accounts for him being a worshiper of the God of Abraham and accounts for his multiple use of the term El Shaddai—translated Almighty—a name for God that Abraham used in Genesis 22:14 (El Shaddai means the Lord will provide).

There are other biblical reasons why I think Job and Moses were contemporaries. The first of Job's friends—Eliphaz—was a son of Esau (Gen. 36:10,11). Eliphaz was one generation older than Job. Therefore, Eliphaz, who rebuked Job, was really a crotchety old uncle who thought his family ties gave him the right to criticize Job.

Also, the second "comforter" was Bildad who was probably the one mentioned as a son of Abraham and Keturah (Gen. 25:5). Bildad would have been a great uncle to Job. (In my home in the South, we would have said a great uncle once removed). Bildad's advanced age (two generations older than Job) would have explained why he was so abrupt with Job.

Many disagree with the Mosaic authorship of Job saying that Job actually wrote the book because of the phrase, *"My eye has seen all [this,]"* (Job 13:1). Whether Job or Moses wrote the book, only God knows for sure. I have given the facts so you can decide.

Moses' Language Ability

Up until the time of Moses the Hebrew language was a crude dialect spoken by Abraham and his family as they communicated to each other. The word Hebrew comes from *habru* a word literally meaning, "on the other side." The Hebrew dialect was spoken by Abraham before he was called by God when he lived on the other side of the Euphrates River. But the Hebrew language is unlike the other Semitic languages spoken in the Near East world in Moses' day. Hebrew was a phonetically-based language. Hebrew letters were based on the sounds that were spoken. The languages of the Egyptians, Chaldeans, etc., the other languages of Moses' day, were based on letters that are sight-picture symbols. These Near East languages did not have letter alphabets, but rather communicated their ideas by drawing images or pictures on paper or stone. Each of the thousands of letters communicates different pictures they had in their mind.

There are 22 letters in the Hebrew alphabet; each letter identifies sounds of the mouth. Today, English is a phonetical language of 26 letters. In contrast, Japanese and Chinese are picture-sight languages based on thousands of picture symbols.

The ancient Phoenicians were the first to develop a phonetical language, i.e., the word phonics comes from Phoenicians. We find the influence of the Phoenician language on the Egyptian culture by researching the tombs of the Egyptians pharaohs. Moses was exposed to the Phoenician influence: *"Moses was learned in all the wisdom of the Egyptians, and was mighty in words and deeds"* (Acts 7:22). As Moses learned the Phoenicians' alphabet and languages, he integrated their phonetical approach to the Hebrew language, his mother tongue. Hence, Moses probably developed and perfected the written Hebrew language.

Moses could have taught Hebrew to Job during their 15 years of overlapping history so that Job wrote the book in Hebrew. However, it is probably more likely that Moses penned the words of Job and later wrote the five books of the Pentateuch.

One last word, while I think the evidence suggests Moses wrote the Book of Job, no one knows for sure who the author is. It's not like Paul's epistles where we know he wrote the books, because he introduced them with his name. Only God knows for sure who the author is, because the Holy Spirit breathed (2 Tim. 3:16) on the human author so that what he wrote is inspired and inerrant. Job is the Word of God, perfect in the original manuscripts, without error.

My Prayer

Lord, thank You for this book
>*That helps me understand why good people suffer*
>*And struggle in this world.*
>*Help me in my struggles.*

Lord, I accept my finiteness,
>*I know I am not perfect;*
>*Yet, I want to live a godly life.*
>*Help me maintain my integrity—*
>*as did Job—in all I say and do.*

>>*Amen.*

Chapter 1

THE ENEMY ATTACKS

Lord, teach me from the Book of Job how to deal with trouble;
>Job was your faithful servant living in the land of Uz,
>He was blameless, upright, and he trusted in You.
Job had seven sons and three daughters,
>And his vast herds indicated he was wealthy.
He lived in a very large house,
>And enjoyed an extensive reputation from
>surrounding neighbors.

The Character of Job

THE Bible presents Job as a historical person, not a myth. "There was a man" (Job 1:11). He lived in the land of Uz, located in the Western part of the Sinai Peninsula (perhaps near Petra). There is a fourfold description of Job in 1:1. *That man was perfect and upright, and one that feared God, and eschewed evil"* (Job 1:1, KJV).

1. "Perfect" is from the word *tam* meaning upright or undefiled. It's a root that means to complete, or finish. This suggests there is nothing lacking in Job's life or actions. Today we would say "well-rounded spiritually" and free of evil intentions toward anyone.

2. "Upright" is from *yashar* meaning to be straight. This describes Job's desire to always do the right thing.

3. "Feared God" is from *yare* meaning reverential trust of God. This is an Old Testament word that meant salvation. From the beginning the reader learns that Job is God's child.

4. "Eschewed evil" is from *suwr* meaning to turn away, to depart, or to remove. Job was not sinlessly perfect, but Job always chose to do the right thing and follow God.

Lord, help me be faithful in times of prosperity;
        Job would pray for his children and
           Sacrifice in case any of them sinned against You.
    Because they invited their brothers and sisters
           To enjoy a sumptuous fast on their birthday,
    Job was concerned a child might sin against You
           So, he sacrificed for them on a regular basis.

Lord, there's much I don't understand in the unseen world;
        When the angels came into Your presence,
        satan came also with them.
    You asked satan why he was there.
        The adversary answered that he had been
        examining the Brethren
        To determine their sincerity and godliness.
    You held up Job as an example of righteousness,
        But the accuser of the brethren criticized You
        For putting a protective hedge about Job.
    Satan claimed Job was righteous because
        He prospered and had many possessions.
    Satan challenged You to take away Job's possessions,
        And he would curse You to Your face.
    So You allowed satan to test Job
        By taking away everything he owned,
        But You wouldn't let satan harm him physically.

"Hedge" is a protective shield that God puts around the person who follows the Lord. A hedge begins when a person worships and serves God, as did Job (Job 1:1,5). Then God blesses the person (Job 1:10). Quickly let it be added that no "good works" can demand God's blessings because some serve God in persecution and suffering.

When God places a hedge around His child, satan is not allowed to touch them without God's permission; then only for a purpose. However, the sin or unbelief of a Christian can remove God's protective hedge (this is not the same as loss of salvation). When the hedge is gone, the person is open to attacks from the evil one.

Lord, satan is a ruthless enemy who hates Your children;
      He hates every good thing that they have.

  A messenger arrived to tell Job an enemy-raiding party
      Stole all his donkeys and oxen, then killed all
      the servants.
  Another messenger arrived simultaneously to tell how lightning
      Killed all his sheep and shepherds.
  A third messenger arrived to tell how
      The Chaldeans stole all the camels and killed
      the servants.
  A fourth messenger arrived to tell that all Job's children
      Were killed when they were feasting together;
      A powerful tornado collapsed the house,
      crushing them to death.

Lord, help me retain my integrity in times of trial;
      Job's faith in You was not shaken,
      But his immense grief was evident to all.
  Job cried, *Naked came I from my mother's womb,*
      And I shall be naked when I die.
  The Lord gave me all things
      And the Lord has taken all things away;
      I praise the name of the Lord.
  Job refused to blame You for his trouble,
      Nor did he sin in his heart against You.
      Amen.

My Prayer

Lord, I need a hedge to protect me,
> *The enemy is powerful and I am weak.*
> *Deliver me from the evil one who would destroy me*
> *And lead me not into temptation that would*
> *overwhelm Me.*
Thank You for past deliverances and protection;
> *I trust in You Who is greater than the enemy of the world.*
> *Amen.*

Chapter 2

THE ENEMY'S SECOND ATTACK

Lord, help me understand how satan constantly attacks me;
> The enemy came into Your presence again with the angels
> And satan said he was still looking to accuse
> Your people.
You pointed out Job still worshiped You in integrity;
> Even though Job lost everything, he remained faithful to You.
Satan said, *"skin for skin,"* if Job lost his health
> He would curse You because of physical troubles, saying;
> *"A man would give up everything to save his skin."*

Lord, help me understand temptations are a way of life;
> You told satan he could take away Job's health,
> Only the enemy couldn't take away his life.
And Job was inflicted with terrible boils from head to toe,

What people of that day called black leprosy.
To get relief, Job sat in ashes to absorb the mucous
    And he scraped himself with broken pottery to deal
    with his pain.
Job's wife mocked him for trying to maintain his integrity;
    She said, *Curse God and die.*
But Job accused her of being godless asking,
    Are we to receive only from God,
    and reject Him when bad days
    or troubles come?
In all his pain, Job did not sin with his mouth,
    But kept his integrity before God.

Lord, help me understand those who try to help me;
    Job's three friends came to see him:
    Eliphaz the Temanite,
    Bildad the Shuhite,
    and Zophar the Naamathite.
They could hardly recognize Job because of his affliction;
    They grieved loudly and were emotionally upset.
Then they sat in silence with Job for seven days;
    His suffering was too great for words.
        Amen.

My Prayer

Lord, prepare me for sickness and any pain that will come
    When I pass from this life into Your presence.
I don't want to suffer, and I'm not good with pain.
    Give me the integrity of Job to worship You in
    Everything that happens to me physically.
        Amen.

Chapter 3

JOB'S LAMENT

JOB is about to speak, this man who had innumerable blessings ripped from him. When Job curses the day he was born, it is not a curse against Jehovah, nor is it a curse against his sickness. Remember in Chapter 1 the birthdays of his children were important. Now Job says his birth date is absolutely the worse thing that has ever happened. His birth date should have promised happiness and fruitfulness but Job has lost hope in having a good life—but not hope in God. He says, *"Why is light given to a man whose way is hidden, and whom God has hedged in?"* (Job 3:23). In this prayer, Job doesn't try to analyze why he is sick; he doesn't try to explain his conditions, nor does he assume sin brought this calamity upon him. Job's opinion is quite different from his three friends who say God has punished him because of his sin. So the three friends don't console Job in his pain, they end up criticizing him.

Lord, help me respond properly to troubles;
> Job denounced the day of his birth,
> Because his life didn't have hope
> that's promised with each new baby.
Job was sorry he was conceived, and he wanted to forget
> That he was born into meaningless suffering.
Job said, Let my birthday become black,
and shrouded in Darkness;
> Don't even let God know about it.
Let a dark cloud overshadow the events,
> And erase it off the calendar so no one will remember.
Don't let anyone rejoice on my birthday
> And let everyone hear words from the pessimist about
> how bad it is.

Don't let the morning stars give any hope to that day,
　　And may the sun not welcome my birth.
Job denounced the opening of his mother's womb,
　　And the fact he was born into all this trouble.

Lord, may I always treasure the breath of life you give;
　　Job asked, Why didn't I die at birth?
　　Why did my mother let me live?
If I had died at birth, I wouldn't be suffering now,
　　But I would be at peace and resting in the grave.
I would be resting with the world's dead rulers,
　　Those who are famous for what they did.
I would be resting with dead wealthy people
　　With their enormous bank accounts and expensive
　　possessions.
Why was I not buried like a still-born baby,
　　Like a child that never saw the light of day?

Why Believer's Suffer

1. Most physical pain and suffering are natural in human life. We get sick because of germs and exposure to bacteria, toxic material; or we come in direct contact with a disease such as AIDS which is transferred by bodily fluids from an infected person. Sometimes we eat improperly or are exposed to adverse weather conditions like rain, extreme heat or cold. There are many things in this world that make both the righteous and ungodly suffer.

2. Some suffering is disciplinary. God uses pain to teach us a lesson (2 Cor. 12:7-10) or to prepare us for greater service (Gen. 50:20).

3. In almost the same emphasis as above, some suffering is to teach important lessons. *"Behold, happy [is] the man whom God corrects; therefore do not despise the chastening of the Almighty"* (Job 5:17). A person goes through the calisthenics of pain to have a stronger body.

4. Some suffering comes from our enemy—satan—to discourage or thwart us (2 Cor. 12:7; Job 1,2).

5. Sometimes God uses suffering as an example to others (James 5:11).

6. Some Christians suffer persecution for their faith and/or godly living (1 Pet. 4:12-19). Jesus predicted His followers would be persecuted and suffer in many ways, even being martyred (John 16:1-4).

7. Some suffering comes through our mistakes, omissions, or hardheaded obstinacy. We speed too fast resulting in an accident. We use a tool wrongly and hurt ourselves. We refuse to take medicine or take proper care of our body—the temple of God.

8. Sometimes we suffer because we are being punished by God. Sin has consequences, and those who violate God's principles suffer pain, loss, or physical damage; not to mention, psychological and social embarrassment (Gal. 6:7,8; 1 Cor. 11:30-32).

Lord, help me understand the finality of death;
> *Job said, In death, the wicked don't trouble anyone*
> *And the weary of this life find rest.*
Those who have been in prison no longer fight,
> *There's no one in the grave to accuse or to curse them.*
> *The rich and the poor are alike in the grave,*
And the slave is free from his master.

Lord, why have You given light to the miserable
> *And life to those who are bitter?*
They search for death, but can't find it;
> *They look for it as the greatest treasure in life.*
They think death is a blessed relief when it finally comes;
> *They actually shout for joy because death is a blessing.*

Lord, why do You give life to those like me with no future?
> *Why are some destined to live in pain?*
I cannot eat because

I continually cry and mourn,
My groans pour out like water.
The thing I feared most has happened to me;
What I dreaded now gives me pain.
I have no peace, no escape and no quietness;
But I only see anguish and trouble in the future.
Amen.

My Prayer

Lord, help me look through all suffering
To see Your hand in my life.
Job was sorry that he was born
Yet You had a purpose for his life;
Help me see Your purpose in my life.
Amen.

Chapters 4:1–5:27

ELIPHAZ'S FIRST COUNSEL

ELIPHAZ was a son of Esau (Gen. 36:10,11), and was the old uncle who visited his distant nephew—Job. When Eliphaz sees Job's wretched condition and realizes that he is an outcast suffering from elephantiasis, he believed that Job's sickness was nothing but the immediate judgment of God upon him. This disease (known then as "black leprosy"), made a person a social outcast and traditionally people of that day believed it was caused by the sin of the victim.

Eliphaz was so "shaken" by the sight of Job that he sat for seven days without saying anything. He was probably debating in his mind how he should respond to Job. Usually comforters come to bless those who are sick, but Eliphaz rationalizes, "How can I bless Job if God has cursed him?" If Eliphaz blessed Job, he would be taking sides with the evil one. So it was Eliphaz's duty to side with God, condemn Job, and forget about giving any sympathy.

The writer wisely includes in this book the opinion of many that sickness is the judgment of God. The way Eliphaz condemns Job is how many people feel about sickness.

Eliphaz claims that his wisdom is the result of ages of thought and experience (Job 15:17-19) and that he has spent his life in study to learn these things (Job 5:27).

Eliphaz also claims that his opinion about Job is right because he had a revelation, a vision (Job 4:12). Eliphaz is arguing that God told him in a vision that Job was wrong.

Finally Eliphaz uses logic, arguing from effect back to cause. He tells Job that his impurity and sin are the cause of all his troubles (Job 4:7-11). Eliphaz wants Job to be quiet rather than expressing his wrath and anger (Job 5:2,3; 6:2,3; 30:24). In conclusion, Eliphaz promises that Job will be restored as soon as he repents and submits to the will of God.

At the end, Eliphaz does not have any human feelings for Job; rather, he can only criticize his nephew.

Lord, help me to understand before I speak;
> Eliphaz finally spoke to Job after seven days
> Because it took him that long to arrive at what he would say.
>> Eliphaz said, *If I tell you what's wrong, you will get mad*
>>> *Yet, I can't keep my opinion to myself.*
>> *Job, you have given moral instruction to many;*

You have strengthened feeble hands.
You have strengthened those who were faltering
 But now misfortune has come to you,
 And you are surprised.
Shouldn't you trust the Lord you fear?
 And shouldn't your integrity be your hope?

Lord, help me to not judge others ignorantly;
 Eliphaz told Job to think about the reasons
 That may have caused his trouble.
Think about how God always judges sin,
 How the Lord even destroys the guiltless.
Those who plough sin in their life
 Reap the whirlwind of God's punishment.
The guilty perish, judged by the breath of God;
 At the blast of His anger, they are consumed.
The lions may growl, the young lions roar,
 And the old lion's teeth are broken;
But lions scatter when there is no prey,
 And God would not have judged you if you had not sinned.

Lord, may I never deceitfully claim to have "miraculous"
  manifestations;
 Eliphaz claimed to have a vision,
  As he said, A word was brought to me silently,
  My ears caught only a whisper of the message.
I received a vision in the night,
 It came to me when other people were sleeping.
I was scared to death when I saw the vision
 And my bones shook uncontrollably in fear.
A spirit passed in front of my face
 And the hairs on my skin stood up.
It stopped in front of me, but I couldn't discern it;
 There was a shadow without form.

Then I heard the voice speak to me,
> *'Can a human man be more righteous than God?*
> *Can a human stand pure before his Creator?*
God knows every one of His servants is a sinner,
> *Even the angels are not perfect.*
How much more sinful are those who live in houses of clay?
> *They are all created out of dust.*
They are crushed as easily as a worm;
> *They can be destroyed between sunrise and sunset.*
They perish forever and no one notices;
> *They die ignorantly not realizing*
> *Their sin has caused their death.'*

Lord, may I not accuse others falsely;
> Eliphaz told Job he had pain because of his sin,
Yell for help, but no one will come to you.
> *You can turn to the angels,*
> *But they won't help you.*
Resentment kills those who won't listen to counsel,
> *And arrogance destroys the ignorant.*

Lord, guard my lips from calling anyone a fool.
> Eliphaz told Job that even a fool could turn to God
> And have momentary success and prosperity
> Just as Job had temporary wealth but lost it all.
The children of fools have no one to help them;
> *They lost their money, possessions and reputation.*
Evil doesn't come from the ground
> *And trouble doesn't come from the earth.*
No, people are born to cause trouble and problems
> *Just as surely as sparks fly upward.*

Lord, may I never give hypocritical advice;
> Eliphaz told Job, *Beg God for forgiveness for your sin;*
Humbly present your case before God

For God is more compassionate than we understand;
    He performs wondrous things without number.
He gives rain to the thirsty fields,
    He sends water to grow our crops.
He raises up those who are humble,
    And lifts to safety those who mourn;
    And God will do the same for you—Job.
But God frustrates the plans of the devious
    So that they fail with their schemes.
God catches the deceivers in their own trap
    And works their plans against them;
    You are guilty because you are being judged.
Schemers grope in the sunlight as though they were blind;
    They see no better in the daylight than in darkness.
God rescues the poor from the enticing words of schemers
    And saves them from their snares.
God gives hope to the poor
    But He breaks the fangs of the wicked.
        Amen.

My Prayer

Lord, help me to study the Bible
    To learn more about You in Scripture.
Keep me from any wrong doctrine that comes
    From nightmares or from thinking I see visions,
When it's not You.

Lord, I will listen for Your still small inner voice
    That says, "This is the way, walk in it."
        Amen.

Chapter 5

EL SHADDAI

ONE of the favorite names for God in the Book of Job is El Shaddai. The name El Shaddai was first revealed to Abraham (Gen. 17:1) and was a primary name for God until Exodus 6:3 when the name LORD (Jehovah) became God's predominant name. Its root is *shad* which means breast. It shows a child getting nourishment and comfort from a mother's breast. So, El Shaddai means God satisfies and comforts us. God reminded Job in his darkest hour of suffering that He would refresh Job and see him through his trials.

El Shaddai also reflects the strong chest of a man to protect and provide for His people. The name is translated *Almighty* in the *King James Bible*, and shows how God strengthens His children. The name El Shaddai occurs 31 times in the Book of Job, reflecting God is our all-sufficient source when we suffer.

Lord, help me see properly the pain of others,
   Eliphaz told Job he would be happy if he repented.
 Happy is the one whom God corrects,
   So don't despise the punishment of El Shaddai.
 Because God gives both wounds and He gives bandages,
   God strikes but He also heals.
 God will rescue you again and again
   So that no evil can harm you.
 God will save you from six disasters;
   Yes, God will deliver you from seven so you're not harmed.
 God will save you from death in famine
   And from the sword in time of war.
 God will protect you from slander

And you won't fear when destruction comes.
You will laugh at judgment
 And wild animals will not scare you.
Your crops will prosper and give a good harvest;
  God will shield you from evil threats. Your home will be safe
  And when you go away, nothing will be stolen from You.
You will live to a ripe old age
  And you will not die before your appointed time.

Lord, don't let me become hardened to hurting people;
  Eliphaz told Job to listen to his advice,
  Repent of his sin that caused his troubles and turn to
God with all his heart,
Then God would restore his prosperity
  And again bless his life.
    Amen.

My Prayer

Lord, it's so easy to judge others;
  Forgive me when I've been critical of people in the past.
Take away any sarcasm from my heart;
  Help me overcome any superiority
  I have toward others.
Help me see my faults,
  Then forgive me as I forgive others.
    Amen.

Chapters 6–7

JOB'S ANSWER TO ELIPHAZ

THIS is Job's first defense against his three accusers. Up until now Job probably didn't know how they would attempt to console him. But Eliphaz deducted that Job is suffering because he had sinned. Job rejects that accusation. Job accuses Eliphaz of being insipid, trivial, and not sincere. Job says that Eliphaz has a false view of God.

Job says their effort is like "flavorless food," the white of an egg, and Eliphaz's consolation makes him lose his appetite (Job 6:6,7). Second, Job says their criticism is so painful that it makes him want to die rather than go on living (Job 6:8-13). Eliphaz has not encouraged Job to overcome his troubles, nor even to endure his pain, but Eliphaz has accelerated a death wish. In the third place, Job feels Eliphaz has eroded his intuitive center. Job feels he can't even trust himself. *"[Is] my help not within me? And is success driven from me?"* (Job 6:13).

The thing that most bitters Job is that the friends on whom he has counted for support are deceitful like a dried up brook (waddi). Instead of giving life-giving water, they make him want to die (Job 6:15-21).

Job notices they are not using honest words, for he asked, "How forceful are right words! But what does your arguing prove?" (Job 6:25). They are not sensitive to his sickness, nor are they sympathizing with Job but using him for their cold, calculated purposes" (Job 6:27).

Job tries to tell his friends that the severity of his punishment is out of proportion with the integrity of his life, but they will not listen to him. Job tells them he has no hope, and that when he lies down to sleep, he looks for the dawn; and with the rising sun he looks to go to sleep the next night (Job 7:3-4). He then ends up by describing how terribly painful is his physical torment.

From this point on, Job will pay little attention to what they say. As a result, Job's comforters will become more exaggerated in their statements to him, rather than offering help and comfort. The chasm grows wider throughout the book.

Lord, Job answered Eliphaz,
>*If my troubles could be weighed*
And my difficulties stacked on a scale,
>*They would be heavier than the sand of the seashore.*
No wonder my words came out rashly
>*And I speak so harshly;*
>*The arrows of El Shaddai have pierced my heart.*
I have been poisoned by my calamities
>*And my fate is worse than death.*

Lord, Job asked a question,
>*Does an animal bray when it has enough food?*
>*Can food be enjoyed without salt?*
>*Do egg whites have any taste?*
Job draws the conclusion, *No!*
>These things caused Job to lose his appetite
>Just as Job's troubles took away his desire to live.

Lord, Job told his friends he has only one desire,
>That God would take away his life.
Then Job would feel consoled
>Because that would end his unending pain.
Then Job said he would be able to rejoice
>Knowing he hadn't denied the Holy One.
Job asked, *Do I have enough strength to keep suffering?*
>*Do I have any hope to keep enduring my troubles?*
Can my body throw off storms like a rock?
>*Am I made of bronze to blunt attacks?*
Job answers his own hypothetical question,
>*No! I am utterly defenseless.*

Lord, Job told his accuser,

> *You should be kind to someone in trouble.*
> *But you are as unreliable as a flood of water*
> > *That runs dry when you run out of words to say.*
> *You're like ice that dams up the streams;*
> > *You'll vanish when the hot weather arrives.*
> *When desert travelers come to drink of you,*
> > *They'll die in the sweltering wilderness*
> > *Because you have no water to give those in trouble.*
> *You have become a dry waddi without life-giving water,*
> > *You saw my calamity and gave me no hope or comfort;*
> > *You have heaped trouble upon my trouble.*

Lord, Job turned to rebuke his friends,

> > *Did I ever ask you to give money to help me?*
> > *Did I ever ask you to save me from the enemy?*
> *Job told Eliphaz, I want a straight answer:*
> > *Tell me what I have done wrong?*
> > *List the sins you say I've committed.*
> *Job explains, If you speak honest words, they'll be forceful,*
> > *But your speech doesn't convince me of anything*
> > *Because you didn't listen to my cry for help.*
> *I have not sinned, and that is the truth;*
> > *Would I lie to your face*
> > *Especially when I'm in this terrible torment?*
> *Quit telling me I'm guilty of sin,*
> > *I've lived by my conscience before God.*
> > > Amen.

Chapter 7

JOB'S ANSWER CONTINUED

Lord, Job told Eliphaz, *Life is like serving in the army,*
>> *Life is long and hard and it's a struggle to stay alive.*
> *Life is like working all day for wages,*
>> *My life's work is drudgery and futility;*
>> *I don't have hope for wages, only more pain and trouble.*
> *When I go to bed, I only hope for the morning;*
>> *When the sun comes up, I only hope to sleep at night.*
> *My skin is full of worms and poison;*
>> *When a scab breaks open, pus runs out.*
> *My days fly swifter than a high-speed gazelle,*
>> *Each day ends without hope.*
> *My life is just one breath at a time;*
>> *I will never see good times again.*
> *You see me now, but not for long;*
>> *Pretty soon I'll die and pass on*
>> *And my life will not come back.*
> *I'm like a passing cloud, gone forever,*
>> *Never to be seen again.*

Lord, Job spoke harshly against his accuser,
>> *I cannot keep quiet while you complain.*
> *I'm not some type of monster you have to guard*
>> *But I am bitter at what you've said.*
> *I try to get some relief by sleeping,*
>> *But your vision scared me to death;*
>> *I don't think God was speaking by your vision.*

I'd rather die than have you comfort me,
  So, leave me alone!

Lord, Job asked his tormentor,
   What is a man that you should care about him?
 You come here every morning looking for my sin,
   You analyze every word I speak looking for mistakes;
   Leave me alone, just for a few minutes.
 Why is my sin so important to you?
   What have I done to make you attack me?
 Why have you come to make my troubles more unbearable?
   Why don't you just forgive my sin?
 If you think I've committed sins you haven't seen,
   Wouldn't your forgiveness help take away my pain?
 But no, you keep accusing me of sins I haven't committed;
   Some day I'll die and be buried in the ground,
   You'll look for me but I will be gone.
    Amen.

My Prayer

Lord, it's hard when people accuse me of things I haven't done.
  I know I'm not perfect,
  But I forgive them their debts
  So they'll forgive me my debts (Matt. 6:12).
Keep me from slander;
  May complaining people not give me
  a negative outlook on life.
   Amen.

Chapter 8:1-22

BILDAD'S FIRST COUNSEL

BILDAD is the second of Job's three friends and is a Shuhite, coming from the area of Shuhan, named for another of the sons of Keturah (Gen. 25:2). Being Abraham's descendent, Bildad, would have known God's people and become acquainted with Job. Family members tend to know their rich relatives. Bildad was the great uncle to his "rich" nephew, Job.

Bildad's three speeches are contained in Job 8, 18, and 25. The content of his speeches is largely an echo of what Eliphaz said, but he somewhat increases the vehemence (Job 8:2; 18:3,4), because he accuses Job of being wrathful and revengeful in the things he is saying.

While Eliphaz implies Job is a sinner, Bildad attributes Job's calamity to his wickedness, and suggests indirectly that his children were destroyed as a punishment of their sin (Job 8:4).

While Eliphaz appealed to logic and the vision he claimed he had from God, Bildad seems to appeal to tradition (Job 8:8-10). He also emphasized the precarious state of the wicked that they are always on the edge of judgment: implying that's where Job is located.

Lord, may I not wrongly attack others;
> Bildad began speaking sarcastically,
>> *How long will you huff and puff?*
>> *Does God twist the truth?*
>> *Does the Almighty turn wrong into right?*
> *Your children were guilty of sin against God*
>> *So they deserved the punishment they got.*
> *If you will earnestly seek God,*
>> *If you will beg for His favor,*
> *If you will live a pure honest life,*

God will restore your home and family.
Even though your beginning was small,
  Your end can be great.

Lord, help me understand the motives of others,
    Bildad appealed to tradition to make his point,
  Ask the previous generations what is right,
      Listen to the wisdom you can learn from tradition.
  Those who were born yesterday know very little,
    Their days are like a passing shadow.
  The ancient elders will tell you the truth;
      They will not be reluctant to tell what is wrong.
      (The elderly Bildad claims to know the truth).
  Can marsh grasses grow where there is no water?
      Can bulrushes live in dry sand?
  No—they die if there is no water to keep them alive,
      And you are dying because you've denied the truth of God.

The godless have no hope because of their sin,
      Everything they count on will crumble;
      They are trusting spider webs to hold them up.
  The godless think their home is secure
      Trying to hold on to their houses,
      But the ungodly will eventually lose everything.
  Job, that's why you lost your possessions and home,
      You are guilty of hidden iniquity.
  The ungodly seem to be strong like a mighty tree
      That prospers in the sunshine
      And spreads its branches out over the ground.
  Its roots go down through the rocks to give it strength
      But it's forgotten when it's cut down.
  Job, that's a picture of your destiny
      When you're cut down; no one will miss you.
      Another tree will grow to replace you.

Lord, keep me from offering sarcastic hope;
> Bildad offers his view of hope after condemning Job.
> *God will not reject a blameless man,*
> > *Nor will He prosper one who sins against Him.*
> *God can give you laughter again,*
> > *Your lips can sing praises and shout for joy.*
> *Then those who have criticized you will be embarrassed*
> > *And you will be vindicated anew.*
> > > Amen.

My Prayer

Lord, give me sensitivity to know when criticism is accurate
> *And help me learn from it.*
> *Give me courage to reject criticism that comes from a hypocrite,*
> > *Or criticism that is wrongly based.*
> *I yield myself to You;*
> *I want to walk humbly with You and grow in righteousness.*
> > Amen.

Chapters 9:1–10:22

JOB'S ANSWER TO BILDAD

JOB begins his answer to Bildad with a question, *"How can man be just with God?"* (Job 9:2, KJV). Job is suggesting Bildad can't answer this question. Then Job said he is blameless; the word Job used is "integrity."

Job never questions the existence of God (9:4-10), his question has to do with whether God has dealt rightly with him (Job 9:12-14). This question by Job is often asked by those in pain, "Why am I suffering?" Pain and suffering don't come from God, He only allows it. Pain comes from our finite body that will eventually die, probably in pain. Pain may come from internal disease, or from external viciousness of other humans.

Job says he would like to summon God into court (Job 9:15,16) to ask, "Why am I suffering?" Yet Job knows, *If I justify myself, mine own mouth would condemn me"* (Job 9:20).

So Job says pain comes on all, *"You cannot judge one's moral quality by his outer appearance"* (Job 9:22-24). Finally, Job knows suffering is universal because he sees others suffering like himself.

Job says life is like a runner (Job 9:25), a ship (Job 9:26), an eagle that kills its prey (Job 9:26). These illustrate that life is brief, precarious, and cruel.

Job wearily maintains his innocence, *"You know that I am not wicked"* (Job 10:7). Yet Job complains that God *"huntest me as a fierce lion"* (Job 10:16, KJV).

Lord, I acknowledge I am not perfect.
>   Job admitted the truth of fallen humanity;
>   How can anyone declare he is perfect before God?
> Job said, *If I could answer God in a courtroom,*
>   *I could never claim to be perfect in His sight.*
> *God's choices are wise; God's ability is mighty,*
>   *No one could ever successfully challenge Him.*
> *God moves mountains without asking anyone,*
>   *They quake because He speaks.*
> *God shakes the earth according to His will;*
>   *The foundations tremble.*
> *God could command the sun not to shine*
>   *And the stars not to shine.*
> *God alone spread the hemisphere in creation,*
>   *He alone can walk on the waves of the sea.*

44

God created the stars—the Great Bear, Orion, the Pleiades;
He made the constellations we can't see.
God's purpose in creation is unsearchable,
We can't count all the things He has done.

Lord, I know You are omnipotently powerful, yet I can't see You;
Job agreed, Yet I can't see the Creator
Nor recognize Him when He passed by.
God sends death to take people away
And no one asks, What are You doing?
God does not withdraw His anger;
The mightiest contenders are crushed by Him.

Lord, You are greater than I can comprehend;
Job said, How can I answer God? How can I argue with God?
Even when I have my integrity
I wouldn't try to answer God;
I would throw myself on His mercy.
Even if I summoned God to the courtroom
He wouldn't listen to my plea of innocence.
God could break me with a storm,
He doesn't need a reason to wound me.
I wouldn't even have time to catch my breath
For God could send the sorrows of this life.
If it's a matter of omnipotent power,
God can do it all.
If it's a matter of justice,
I can't challenge Him.
Even if I proclaim my innocence,
I fall short of God's standards.
Even if I said, I am innocent, it means
I don't really know my own heart.
So the story of life is very simple:
The wicked have troubles just like the innocent;

Life is the same for all God's creatures.
When disaster suddenly brings death,
 The innocent along with the wicked dies.
Yet, this life is controlled by wicked people
 And God let's them do what they want;
 He let's them break every law.

Lord, I know that I am finite
 And life isn't fair;
 Job said life is like three things:
  Life goes by swiftly like a sprint runner,
  Life comes apart like a boat made of reeds,
  Life swoops downs to eat you up like a hungry eagle,
 Life is brief, precarious, and cruel.

Lord, help me not complain
 When trouble comes
 Because Job said, *If I decide to stop complaining*
  And start living as though nothing is wrong,
I'll still suffer with my pain,
 And I'll know I'm not perfect in God's sight.
I'd be condemned by a perfect God,
 So why should I keep quiet and act like normal People?
Even if I washed myself in new fallen snow
 And scrubbed my hands with lye,
I'd probably fall into a muddy ditch
 And I'd be filthy again.

Lord, I know You don't do things as humans;
 Job admitted, *God is not mortal*
 So he couldn't argue with Him in a trial.
If only I had a mediator to plead my case
 Who could bring me to God;
 But in this life there is none.
I need a mediator to deal with my punishment

Then I could speak to God without fear,
But I can't do it in my strength.
Amen.

❦═╪ ╪═❦

Chapter 10

JOB'S WEARINESS

Lord, I sometimes get tired of all my struggles;
        Job agreed, *I am worn out*
        So I keep complaining.
   I want to tell God, 'Don't keep punishing me,
        Let me know what I've done wrong.'
   Is there a purpose to my suffering?
        What advantage is there in my pain?
   God, why do You allow me such agony
        And You let the wicked have a good life?
        You made me who I am.
   God can You see me as others see me?
        Can You feel for me as other mortals?
   Why do You ignore my pain
        As others in life don't care about my suffering?
   God You know I am not guilty
        Yet, there is no relief for my agony.

Lord, help me to see Your great plan for my life;
        Job said, *God You formed me with Your hands,*
        You can destroy me when You want.

God, You formed me from the dust of the ground
    And one day I'll return to dust.
God You were present when I was conceived,
    You saw me become skin and bones.
God by Your grace, You gave me life;
    You preserved me to this minute.
Yet, You had plans for me I didn't know about,
    You watch to see if I'll sin against You
    And You're ready to punish me when I sin.
If I have sinned against You
    Then I deserve my suffering. But I know I am innocent,
    Yet I still suffer in pain. I can stand before You blameless
    Because I know I have lived in integrity.
Yet, You allow pain to hunt me like a tiger,
    Pain is one way Your power is shown.
I can't get away from my predicament;
    My pain keeps growing
    Like troops attacking me, wave after wave.

Lord, I have difficulty knowing why anyone suffers;
    Job questioned, *God why was I brought from the womb?*
Why didn't You let me die at birth
    Then I wouldn't have this suffering;
    I could have gone from the womb to death?
I only have a little time left
    So I want you false comforters to leave me alone
    And go away.
When you leave, I'll be happier
    Before I go to my grave.
It is a land that is dark as night itself
    Where even the light is black like midnight.
        Amen.

My Prayer

Lord, Job has many questions
            But he never denied Your power and sovereignty over his life.
I acknowledge Your control over all things—
even blessings and pain.
I praise You for the good things in my life
            When pain and sorrow come.
Teach me to praise You, even in trouble.
                        Amen.

Chapter 11:1–20

ZOPHAR'S FIRST COUNSEL

ZOPHAR, the youngest of the three friends is called "the Naamathite" (Job 2:11). He is from Naamah, six miles south of Lod, in Judah's Negev Desert. He has the youthful attributes of sarcasm and bitter criticism. Zophar thinks Job is disrespectful of God—a complaining old man.

Zophar doesn't bother with an introduction, perhaps because his two friends, Eliphaz and Bildad, have already spoken. Zophar doesn't cite a night vision like Eliphaz, nor does he appeal to tradition like Bildad; he uses worldly wisdom and common sense to condemn Job.

Zophar is a dogmatist, everything is either right or wrong, black or white. So he assumes Job is not innocent but guilty.

Lord, I want my love for You to go beyond my words;
　　　　　Zophar jumped into his accusation,
Job, you talk too much.
　　　　　I can't remain silent while you babble on,
　　　　　　No one is ever proven innocent by much talking.
Is your ceaseless talking supposed to shut us up?
　　　　　You ought to be ashamed for mocking God.
You claim your words are right,
　　　　　You tell God you are upright in your heart.
I wish God would talk so He would answer you;
　　　　　He would tell you what is right.
Doesn't that make common sense to you?
　　　　　God is punishing you for your guilt;
　　　　　Your suffering is less than you deserve.

Can you understand the depths of God?
　　　　　Can you discover the mysteries of El Shaddai?
God's ways are higher than the heavens,
　　　　　His purposes are deeper than Hell.
God's plans are wider than the universe
　　　　　And broader than the seas.
If God allows a person to be called in judgment
　　　　　Or if He allows one to be put into prison,
　　　　　Who can stop Him?
God knows those who are not true;
　　　　　He writes a record of their sins
　　　　　So God knows your heart, Job.

Lord, help me to understand the way You do things
　　　　　For Zophar said, *No human knows everything*
　　　　　　Any more than a donkey can give birth to a man.
If you will straighten out your heart before God,
　　　　　If you will lift your hands to Him,
If you will repent of your iniquity,

And quit living in a house of sin,
Then, when you seek God, you will find Him
And you will be free from your pain.
Then your misery will finally come to an end
Like a flood, your troubles will pass away.
Your life will be bright like the sun
And your darkness will be like the morning.
You will have courage because there is hope
And you can sleep securely.
Many will come again to seek your advice
But the wicked will not listen to you.
The wicked have no hope;
They have nothing but despair.
Amen.

My Prayer

Lord, keep me from being like Zophar
Who judges others wrongly.
Teach me to listen to people and evaluate them according to truth.
I don't want to hurt people,
So help them become strong in faith.
Amen.

Chapters 12–14

JOB'S ANSWER TO ZOPHAR

JOB doesn't single out Zophar in his answer, but Job speaks to all three of his counselors because each has had their say. So Job answers them sarcastically, *"I realize you know everything"* (Job 12:2, TLB). Then Job boasts, *I know a few things myself—you are no better than I am* (Job 12:3, author's translation). But then Job lapses back into self pity, *"I am one mocked"* (Job 12:4).

In chapter 12:7-25, Job repeats what the friends said about God, proving his belief in God is not the problem. Job has never doubted God's power, so Job gives his own views of God (Job 12:13-25).

At the beginning of chapter 13 Job defends himself, *"I am not inferior to you"* (Job 13:2). Job says his friends have not said any new thing and they've failed miserably to find out what is his problem.

Job turns his attention to God (Job 13:13-28) and makes a faith-statement, *"Though He slay me, yet will I trust Him. Even so, I will defend my own ways before Him"* (Job 13:15).

Lord, help me to be truthful when verbally attacked
> As Job answered his three friends,
>> *You think you know everything*
>>> *And that all wisdom will die with you.*
>> *I can think rationally and I know a lot of things;*
>>> *You three are no better off than I am.*
>> *Everyone knows what I've been saying all along;*
>>> *I ask God for help in my suffering*
>>> *But I've become a laughing stock to them.*
>> *Yes, I have kept my integrity before God*

And people ridicule and mock me.
The rich ridicule those in trouble
    And despise the poor because they have nothing;
    Yet, in spite of their prejudice, the rich prosper.
The thief also prospers,
    Even those who despise God prosper.
So the three of you are wrong;
    A person doesn't have to be righteous to prosper;
    You provoked God with your silly talk.
Go ahead, ask the dumbest animal,
    Then study the birds flying in the sky;
    Also, look at the fish of the sea.
Every one of them knows
    God's hand has created everything.
Just as my mouth knows what food it tastes,
    So my mind knows the truth it hears.
Older men—like me—may be wise,
    But all true wisdom comes from God;
    He alone knows what we should do.

God has great strength;
    When He destroys something,
    No one is able to rebuild it.
When God withholds the rain,
    The earth becomes a desert.
When God sends the rain,
    A flood destroys all within its path.
When God limits a man,
    He cannot escape.
With God is all wisdom and all strength;
    He does what He wills with deceivers and the deceived.
God can take away the good judgment of counselors
    So that their decisions are illogical.
God can take away the judgments of kings

So that their office is taken from them.
God can disgrace the strong men of the king
    And take away their weapons in which they trust.
God can silence the trusted counselors
    Which He should do with your three comforters.

Lord, I recognize Your sovereignty
        As Job said,
You make light to overcome darkness
        And You shine light in the blindness of men.
You lift nations and You put them down;
        You let nations conquer, and You let them collapse.
You take away the wisdom of leaders
        So they stagger in the wilderness without a path.
They search for light in the darkness
        And stumble as a drunkard.
                Amen.

Chapter 13

JOB'S FAITH IN GOD

IN Chapter 13 Job directs the attention of his three friends toward God, just as he did at the end of Chapter 12. But in this chapter, Job expresses his faith in God.

Lord, I want to deal with my critics
        Just as Job answered his three counselors.

Job said, *I have seen the things you describe*
   So I know what you are trying to do to me.
I have as much learning as you do;
   You are not wiser than I am.
I want to talk directly to El Shaddai,
   I want to explain to Him my case;
   Apparently you three have not understood my case.
You are telling me things that are not true;
   As teachers, you have failed the course you teach.
Keep quiet, and don't show your ignorance;
   Listen to what I have to say.

Lord, may I learn how to answer my critics from Job;
   Job focused his friends on the person of God.
Don't try to defend God with your counsel
   Because you are dishonest, you don't tell the truth.
You should be objective when talking about God,
   But you twist the truth about Him,
   Giving your false interpretation of El Shaddai.
You think you are presenting the truth from God;
   Be careful God doesn't find out the errors you're saying.
You cannot mislead God like you try to mislead me.
   You will be judged by God for your hypocrisy.
Doesn't the thought of a holy God scare you?
   Be careful God doesn't judge you for your slander.
Your arguments are like burned out ashes
   Blown away by the wind. Your reasoning has crumbled
Like a broken clay pot that shatters into pieces.

Lord, teach me to look beyond my critics to see You.
   Job told his comforters, "Be quiet."
I will tell you the truth as it is
   And I will take my punishment
   If I am wrong and you are right.

I will stand on my faith in God;
> *I am ready for what comes my way.*
I will take responsibility for my life
> *But I'll believe and say what I think.*
Though God may slay me,
> *Yet I will trust Him*
> *And I will affirm my faith in God.*
God is my salvation
> *But you hypocrites will be judged by Him.*
In my integrity, I believe in God;
> *If I were not, He'd cast me out of His presence.*

Lord, may I have strong faith like Job
> Who told his three counselors, *Hear me out,*
> *I will prove my innocence. You haven't proved me wrong;*
I would keep silent if you did.

Lord, my prayer is what Job said,
> *O God I want You to do two things for me.*
First, remove Your hand of affliction from me
> *And don't torment me with this suffering.*
Second, invite me into Your presence
> *So You will see my faith and integrity.*
If I have done anything wrong,
> *Show me my sin and transgression.*
Why have You hidden Your face from me?
> *Why have You treated me like an outcast?*
I am as worthless as a dry leaf or as dead grass;
> *Why am I suffering?*
My feet are chained and I am in prison;
> *I am afflicted with this torture.*
I am as useless as rotten wood;
> *I am like a moth-eaten coat.*
> > Amen.

My Prayer

Lord, I don't want to hide anything from You;
Show me any hidden sin.
Forgive me for the wrong I do intentionally,
And for secret sins I do unintentionally.
Cleanse me by the blood of Jesus Christ
And restore me to intimate fellowship with You.
Amen.

Chapter 14

SUFFERING

Lord, I know there is much suffering in the world.
  Job said, *"Those born of woman only have a few days,*
  And their life is filled with suffering."
  We are born with the beauty of a new flower
  But quickly we are cut down and die.
  We are like shadows that creep across the ground,
  Then we disappear as though we had not been here.

Lord, help me to make my days count in this short life.
  Job said, *You three friends know life is frail,*
  What more do you expect of me?
  Those born in iniquity cannot be perfect,
  So I'm not sinless, but I can live without blame.

You, Lord, have determined the years we should live,
  And You know when we will die;
  We will not live longer than You decree.

Lord, may I rebuke people with a kind spirit, as Job said;
  So give me a little room to be human
  And quit looking at me as though I'm guilty.
We are all employees of God;
  Let's finish the task He's given us in life.
When a tree is cut down
  The roots can sprout again.
But there must be water to give it life
  So it can grow into a new tree.
When a person breathes his last and dies
  Where are they when their life is gone?
As water evaporates in the hot sun
  And as steam disappears when there is no rain,
  So a person dies, is buried and is gone.
They will not awake or return from the grave
  Until Heaven passes away
  And the resurrection gives them new life.

Job prayed, *O hide me in the grave*
  And keep me there until the resurrection
  So I can rid myself of this agony.
I know You have an appointed time for me to die
  And I am ready to go,
  But think of me in the final day.
Because righteous mortals die, so they can live again,
  This gives me hope in suffering and death.
When You call for me in death, I will answer;
  Then You'll know my integrity
  And my sin will no longer be a question.
When mountains crumble and rocks tumble,

When water wears away the stone and the earth erodes,
Then the hope of the resurrection comes.

Lord, You let death overtake all people
And the body rots away to nothing.
In death no one knows what happens to their children,
They leave this earth in pain and grief.
Amen.

My Prayer

Lord, I know I will die—as all people die,
But I have trouble handling pain and fear the unknown;
Help me to die well when the final chord is sounded
For I know I'll be raised in the last day
with a new transformed body.
Amen.

Chapter 15

ELIPHAZ'S SECOND RESPONSE

ELIPHAZ is irritated because he feels Job is blasphemous against God (Job 15:4). He says that every time Job speaks, he reflects the sin in his heart (Job 15:4,5) and since no man is completely cured, Job should confess that he is a sinner and take responsibility for all his sickness (Job 14:15).

Finally, Eliphaz describes the eternal fate of the wicked (Job 15:20-35).
He says that Job is suffering because he is wicked.

Eliphaz says Job will continue to suffer because he refuses to admit that
he is a sinner.

Lord, help me be kind when friends argue
>As when Eliphaz sarcastically answered Job.
>>*If you are as wise as you claim,*
>>>*Why are your words so foolish?*
>>>*You are full of the east wind that is hot air.*
>>*What good is all your talking*
>>>*When you don't know what you're saying?*
>>*You have no fear of God*
>>>*And you don't know how to pray to God.*
>>*You are justifying your sin*
>>>*And you deceive yourself.*
>>*I don't have to condemn you,*
>>>*Your speech proves you are guilty.*

Lord, help me not retaliate against sarcasm
>Just as Job had to listen to Eliphaz.
>Eliphaz asked if Job were the first person born,
>>Or if he was born before the hills were created.
>>*Do you think God speaks only to you?*
>>>*Do you think you're smarter than everyone?*
>>*What insights do you think you have*
>>>*And what do you know that we don't?*
>>*The three of us are older and wiser than you;*
>>>*We are older than your father.*
>>*Why don't you respect us and listen to us*
>>>*As you would your father?*

Lord, what can I do when my friends
>Misunderstand the ways You work in this world?

Eliphaz asked, *Why don't you let God comfort you;*
      Are you hiding a secret sin?
What has blinded you to the truth?
      Why are you looking the other way?
Your stupid words and arguments prove
      You have turned against God.
What person goes through life without sinning
      And who is perfect and righteous?
Even the heavens are not clean;
      God can't even trust His angels.
So how much more corrupt is a sinful person
      Who always seeks his selfish pleasures?

Lord, teach me not to argue with my friends.
      Because Eliphaz had more experience,
      He demanded Job should listen to him.
Wise people have been my teachers
      And they learned their wisdom from their fathers.
God gave the earth to our forefathers
      Not to these strangers who are moving in.

Lord, help me not to condemn my friends
      As Eliphaz falsely accused Job
      Of suffering in pain because of his sin.
Wicked people are tortured in this life,
      They are scared to death all the time;
      Even in prosperity they fear the destroyer.
Wicked people are scared of the darkness,
      They think they'll be killed.
They are always hanging on to their money
      Thinking they'll end up in poverty.
They know the darkness of death is coming
      So they are constantly terrified.
They clench their teeth at God

And dare the Almighty to judge them.
With their fleshly weapons of war,
    They want to fight against God.
Job, you are that foolish man
    Who won't admit he's wrong;
    You are fighting against God.

Lord, give me a humble spirit about hurting people
    Not as Eliphaz who criticized Job because he lost everything.
Wicked rich people blind themselves with money
    And think it will protect them.
But their houses crash in around them
    And the world they build also collapses,
    As did your wealth disappear.
The wicked rich will not endure;
    Their money will slip through their fingers
    And their possessions will disappear.
They can't escape darkness;
    The flames will lick about them
    And the breath of God will destroy them.
They are deceived who trust in self effort,
    They are only fooling themselves;
    They have no reward beyond the grave.
The wicked shall die before they are ready;
    What will his possessions do for him then?
They shall be like green grapes
    Picked too early, only to spoil.
They shall be like an olive tree
    That sheds its flowers
    So no olives grow on the tree.
The ungodly will not have anything in death
    Because the flames will burn everything up
    Just as you—Job—have lost everything.
Evil people think up evil to satisfy their flesh,

It all comes out of an evil heart;
That's your problem, Job.
Amen.

My Prayer

Lord, may I never wrongly accuse a fellow Christian of sin,
Especially when I don't know all the facts.
May I listen to hurting people, be kind to them,
And pray for them.
Give me a considerate heart.
Amen.

Chapters 16–17

JOB'S SECOND ANSWER TO ELIPHAZ

JOB exchanges insults with his three friends. They say Job is a sinner; he says, *"What miserable comforters you are"* (Job 16:2). Job is not looking for their pity; he wants them to feel his righteous indignation because he feels an injustice has been done to him. We the readers know the injustice comes from satan himself.

Lord, give me the patience of Job to endure criticism
And help me answer with a patient spirit.
Job told Eliphaz, *I've heard this stuff before,*
You're a bunch of lousy comforters.

Is there no end to your constant criticism?
    What motivates you to keep up your attacks?
I could criticize you if I were in your place;
    Also, I could describe your sin eloquently
    Or share my negative opinion of you.

But that's not what I would do;
    I would say things to help you,
    I would try to ease your grief.
But you three counselors haven't helped me,
    I still am grieving over my loss;
    It doesn't help when I have to defend myself.

Lord, help me deal with critics
    When it's my time to suffer.
Job told his critics, *You have stomped on me*
    And said I have destroyed my family
    Because of my sin.
You say I am a skeleton, just skin and bones
    Which proves I am a sinner.
You say God hates me;
    He's eating me alive
    And is tearing me apart because of my sin.

Lord, help me deal with public criticism as Job
    Who told his critics,
Everyone laughs and makes fun of me,
    They constantly take jabs at me.
Everyone has turned against me,
    They say God has thrown me to the dogs
    And delivered me into the hands of the executioner.
In my integrity I know I have not sinned
    But I don't understand why I'm suffering.

Lord, help me to look beyond my suffering,
> Help me understand Your plan for my life.

Job said, *I was minding my own business*
> *Yet God allowed the destroyer to attack me.*

I became a target for the evil one
> *Who attacked me with vengeance;*
> *My blood spilt on the ground.*

He attacked me again and again
> *With an unrelenting assault.*

Now I sit in sackcloth and ashes,
> *My body is ravaged with pain.*

My face is tired of weeping
> *And my black eyes look like I'm dying.*

Yet, my hands are free from violence
> *And my prayer is pure.*

Lord, teach me how to pray when I suffer
> As Job prayed in the valley of the shadow of death.

Job prayed, *The grave hasn't covered me yet;*
> *I'm not dead,*
> *I'm still continually praying for a miracle.*

Everyone in Heaven knows my good witness
> *And I need an intercessor before the throne*
> *Pleading my case before God.*

But my three friends don't pray or plead for me,
> *Even when I ask sincerely for their help with tears.*

I need an arbitrator between me and God
> *As a man pleads for his neighbor.*
> Amen.

My Prayer

Lord, give me the patience of Job to endure suffering.
Also, I need his wisdom to endure the sarcasm of critics.
Lord, give me a sweet answer to my critics
And help me look to You in suffering
As did Job in his pain.
Amen.

Chapter 17

HELP ME

Lord, help me be as strong as Job
     When I face the pain of death's river.
Job prayed, *My spirit is broken*
     And I'm about to die.
These three mockers sit all around me
     And I can see bitterness in their eyes.
You must defend me, O God,
     Because no one else will take my side.
The minds of my three friends are blinded to the truth;
     Don't let them get the best of me.
They have flattered me to my face
     But their angry hearts denounce me;
     Their children will be just as blind.

66

Lord, I don't understand why You let righteous Job suffer
   Just as I'll probably not understand
   Why I'll suffer in the future.
  Job said, *God, why have You let people mock me*
    And spit in my face?
I am almost blinded with my tears
   And I'm a skinny bag of bones.
The upright are angry because of what's happened to me;
   The average person is angry at my three friends.
The righteous people will still believe in You
   And those with clean hands will grow in spirit.

Lord, help me answer my critics with kindness
   As Job told his three critics,
Turn around and look at me,
   I don't see an honest man among you.
My days are almost over,
   And my life-dreams are crushed.
You critics don't know the difference between night and day;
   You are blinded to the truth.
You say light is coming
   But I'm going to a dark grave.
I might as well call the grave my home
   And the worms my provider.
Where then is my hope in this pain?
   Who can find some hope to give me in this world?
Will you three comforters follow me into the grave
   To see if I have found my hope?
     Amen.

My Prayer

Lord, it's hard to see any good thing coming from my pain,
But help me trust in You until the day I die.
And if I die with pain, keep my hope strong in You.
Amen.

Chapter 18

BILDAD'S SECOND SPEECH

BILDAD doesn't begin kindly and he ignores Job's plea in the last chapter for sympathy. Bildad lashes out at Job, "How long till you put an end to words?" (Job 18:2). He accuses Job of insulting the intelligence of his three counselors. Then Bildad continues calling Job a sinner, giving a severe picture of those who refuse to repent, "He is driven from light into darkness, and chased out of the world" (Job 18:18).

Lord, keep me from being calloused to the hurting
        As Bildad who attacked Job asking,
    How long will you keep justifying yourself?
        When you wise up, we'll talk.
    Do you think your three counselors
        Are as stupid as dumb animals?
    You can split hairs all you want,
        But you won't change anything on earth;
        Not one rock will be moved.

It's still clear; the light of the wicked goes out
And sparks in a fire will die;
And you, Job, are being punished for your sin.
The lamp in your house will go out
And glowing embers in your fireplace will become black.
Your wickedness will destroy your confident swagger
And your scheme will collapse.

You, like the wicked, will be ensnared in a trap.
A rope will grab you by your foot;
When the noose tightens, you'll not get away.
Dangers surround the sinner on every side;
It's waiting to eat you alive.
Suffering wants to make a meal of you;
Destruction will consume the sinner.
Disease already is eating your skin
And death is gradually devouring you.
All your arguments will be ripped to shreds
And you'll be dragged terrified before the destroyer.
Strangers will live in your earthly home
But you'll be like ashes, burning in brimstone and sulfur.
Your roots below will dry up and rot,
Your branches above will wither.
All memory of you will be erased,
No one will even know you ever lived.
You will be thrown out of the light
And you'll be cast into eternal darkness.
You will not have a son or posterity,
Your line will be snuffed out.
People in the West are astonished at your fate,
People in the East are horrified.
Everyone will remember you were a wicked man,
They will say you rebelled against God.
Amen.

My Prayer

Lord, may I never become so angry that
I accuse anyone of the things Bildad said about Job.
May I have a kind spirit and may I have
Words of kindness for distressed people.
Amen.

Chapter 19

JOB'S REPLY TO BILDAD'S SECOND ATTACK

JOB continues his defense that he made previously. To Job, their attitude is incomprehensible. He strongly defends his innocence.

Lord, help me never give into pressure when
    I know I am right.
Job robustly defended himself saying,
    How long will you irritate me?
    How long will you keep up your attacks?
You've assaulted me ten times with your accusations,
    You ought to be ashamed of yourselves.
Even if I've got hidden sin
    That is none of your business.
You've taken a pious attitude about my suffering

And you use my suffering to prove your point.
It's not my sin that's done this to me,
   It's all within God's sovereignty;
   He's put me in this hole for a reason.

Lord, help me see your great purpose in suffering
   And help me learn when I have trials.
Job cried out, *When I yell for help*
   No one seems to hear me;
   Life is not fair.
God has me pinned up behind a fence,
   It's too dark to see any escape route.
God has stripped me of my position and respect,
   He's taken away all the authority I had.
God has broken down all my defenses,
   He has uprooted me like a tree;
   It is finished, I have no hope.
God seems to be angry with me;
   He treats me like an enemy
   And sends attackers to destroy me.

Lord, I know it's easy to complain;
   Keep me from accusing You of wrongdoing.
Job prayed, *God has kept my brothers*
   From helping me in my troubles;
   He won't let my friends come to my rescue.
My relatives have let me down,
   My close friends have forsaken me.
Those living in my house treat me like a stranger,
   My servants won't even attend to me.
When I call for my staff,
   They won't come
   Even when I beg for help.
My wife rejects me because I have bad breath,

71

My sores are repulsive to children,
    And they laugh at me.
All my close friends turn their backs on me,
    Those I love have turned away.
I'm nothing more than skin and bones,
    I stay alive by the skin of my teeth.

Lord, when I reach out for help in my hour of trials,
    Send someone to help me.
Job asked his three friends for help,
        I need your comfort, not your criticism.
Why are you causing me grief?
        Hasn't God given me enough grief?
I wish my defense were written in a book
        Or carved on a monument
        So everyone would know eternally.
Oh, that everyone would realize I trust God;
        I know that my Redeemer lives
        And that in the resurrection I'll stand on this earth.
After my body decays in the grave,
        In my flesh I'll see God.
I'll stand before God and see Him with my eyes;
        This is my only hope.
If you keep accusing me of evil
        You three will suffer the punishment
        That you wish for me.
                    Amen.

My Prayer

Lord, give me the deep conviction of Job
    About the resurrection
    And hope of Heaven.

I'm not ready to die;
  I have a lot of things I want to do on earth.
But when it comes my time to die
    Give me the faith of Job.
    Help me look confidently beyond the grave to see You in Heaven.
      Amen.

❦━✢ ✢━❦

Chapter 20

ZOPHAR'S SECOND SPEECH

ZOPHAR ignores the lofty statement of faith by Job that *"I know my Redeemer lives."* Zophar thinks the only thing Job has done is to insult him. *"I have had to endure your insults"* (Job 20:3, NLT). So Zophar replies, *"But now my spirit prompts me to reply"* (Job 20:5). Zophar still thinks Job had his wealth taken from him because he is wicked. Then Zophar concludes Job *"will perish forever like his own refuse"* (Job 20:7).

Lord, may I listen for faith in other people;
    Not ignore them as Zophar ignored Job when he said,
  You make me angry with your rebuttals,
    I've endured your drivel long enough;
    Now I'm going to tell you what I really think.
  Don't you know that from the very beginning
    The wicked prosper for only a short time?
  Just as you prospered but lost everything,
    The ungodly are not happy very long.
  The wicked man thinks he is the biggest thing in the world,

He thinks his head reaches to Heaven.
But the ungodly disappear like garbage;
His friends ask, 'Where did he go?'
He is like a night dream that is forgotten,
Like a thought that is fleeting;
No one will see him any more.
His children will beg for food,
They will have to pay back his debts.
The wicked may have been a young man
But his bones rot in the desert.

Lord, help me listen when people confess their faith
And help me look for their strengths, not their failures.
Zophar thought Job was suffering because of his sin
So he said, *Wickedness tastes sweet in your mouth.*
You savor its delicious taste, you roll it on your tongue;
You keep it in your mouth to enjoy its flavor.
Yet your wickedness makes you sick to your stomach;
It's like a snake's venom that will kill you.
Your wickedness is eating up your wealth,
You vomit your sin up, but it's still there.
Your money is like the poison of asps,
The viper's fangs will kill you.

Lord, Zophar had a mean spirit,
Give me love for all people.
Zophar said, *You will never again enjoy the rivers*
Even when streams flow with honey and cream.
You'll have to give away money, the money you worked for;
You won't get to enjoy any of it.
Your hard work will not be rewarded,
Your wealth will not give you any joy.
Because you have oppressed the poor,
You've taken away their homes.

Because your greed is unquenched,
> *You've never been satisfied with what you got.*
You eat up everything in sight because of
your sin and callousness,
> *You've lost your wealth and health.*

Lord, Zophar didn't understand Job so he criticized him;
> He prayed, *May God give Job a belly full of pain.*
May God rain trouble on Job,
> *For the trouble he planned for other people.*
When arrows are pulled from Job's body,
> *May they sparkle with his blood*
> *Telling Job he's dying.*
May his treasures be lost in the darkness,
> *And may a forest fire destroy everything he has.*
May Heaven reveal Job's guilt
> *And may the earth agree by washing away*
> *everything that he has;*
> *This is the way God deals with sin.*
> Amen.

My Prayer

Lord, the prayer of Zophar was cruel and wrong,
> *Keep me from wrongly judging anyone.*
Lord, You are the only One who can judge anyone.
> *When You come to judge me, be merciful.*
> *Amen.*

Chapter 21

JOB'S SECOND ANSWER TO ZOPHAR

JOB directs his answer to all three comforters, telling them both the wicked and righteous prosper all their life until they are buried in peace. And on the other hand, some righteous and wicked both suffer, so the three comforters are wrong when they say Job is suffering because of his sin. Job asks, *"How then can you comfort me with empty words, since falsehood remains in your answers?"* (Job 21:34).

Lord, help me answer my critics carefully
>> As Job answered Zophar, saying,
> *Listen to every word that I say*
>> *So you won't misunderstand what I mean.*
> *When you know how God deals with people*
>> *Then you can continue your mocking, if you wish.*
> *My complaint is with the way people react,*
>> *I have reason to be short tempered;*
>> *I'm not complaining with the way God treats me.*
> *When you look at me, you'll be shocked*
>> *So hide your eyes with your hands.*
> *When I realize what's happened to me,*
>> *I'm stunned and I tremble with fear.*

Lord, help me present the truth to blinded people
>> As Job clearly presented his case to Zophar saying,
> *Do not some wicked people grow to a ripe old age?*
>> *And don't some get wealthy and have good health?*
> *They see their children prosper*
>> *And they enjoy their grandchildren.*
> *Their houses are safe from thieves and destruction,*

God does not seem to punish all the wicked in this life.
Their businesses succeed and become larger,
        They enjoy the fruit of their labors.
Their little children laugh and play around the home,
        There is the sound of happiness in the home.
They spend their days enjoying their life
        And they die a peaceful death.
These are the same wicked who reject God saying,
        'Leave us alone, we won't follow You.'
These wicked sarcastically ask, 'Who is El-Shaddai
        That we should obey and serve Him?' They ask,
'What advantage is there for us to pray?
        Why should we pray to God?'
Job concluded, *Don't the wicked prosper?*
        It doesn't seem the sinner always suffers,
        You three are wrong in your arguments.
The wicked seem to get away with doing wicked things,
        They are not punished each time they sin.
God seems to let some of them get away with sin,
        They just bounce along like straw in the wind.
Some foolishly say, 'God will at least punish their children,'
        But each one is accountable for his sin;
        Their children are not punished for their father's iniquity.
Each one will suffer for his wrong doing,
        El Shaddai will eventually judge the sin of each.

Lord, help me see the big picture before answering
        As Job said to Zophar,
No one can teach God anything,
        He knows perfectly how to deal with everyone.
One person gets very rich and dies in perfect health,
        Another dies poor, never having had an easy life.
Both are buried in the earth,
        Both pass from this life and are gone.

Job then confronted his three counselors,

I know what you're thinking,
You're plotting a scheme against me.
You will tell me about rich people who lost everything,
You say it was because of their wickedness.
But, everyone knows rich people don't have it hard,
Punishment by-passes them.
No one ridicules the rich to his face,
No one punishes him for what he has done wrong.
When the rich are buried
Everyone shows up for their funeral.
The earth receives his body just as sweetly
As it receives the poor.
No, you three are wrong in your logic;
God does not punish all the wicked rich,
Your words are no comfort to me.

Amen.

My Prayer

Lord, help me remember that You don't punish a person on this earth,
Your judgment comes after death.
Then every person will be condemned for their rebellion against You.
Thank You that Christ died for my sin and that I face
no condemnation after death.

Amen.

Chapter 22

ELIPHAZ'S THIRD COUNSEL

ELIPHAZ began immediately attacking Job; no niceties here. Eliphaz does not believe Job is being tested for his integrity (Chapters 1,2), therefore he has only two alternatives. First, God is unjust, and to Eliphaz that is impossible. Second, Job is unrighteous and to Eliphaz this was the answer. So Eliphaz began a new attack with four rhetorical questions, each suggesting Job is guilty.

Lord, You have always dealt justly with everyone,
> But Eliphaz didn't understand Your ways when he asked Job,
>> *Can your actions help God in any way?*
>> *No! Your actions benefit only yourself?*
>> *Is El Shaddai pleased when you try to act righteous?*
>> *That would make no difference to God.*
>> *Is God punishing you severely*
>>> *Because you never reverence Him?*
>> *Is not your wickedness great*
>>> *And your sin without limits?*

Lord, I don't want to wrongly accuse my friends of sin
> Like Eliphaz did of Job, when he asked,
>> *Did you lend money to a friend*
>>> *Then keep his clothing that you took as collateral?*
>> *Did you refuse to give water to a tired traveler*
>>> *Or a meal to a homeless vagrant?*
>> *You were a wealthy land owner*
>>> *Who was respected and powerful.*
>> *You refused to contribute to widows*
>>> *And you sent orphans away empty.*

You're surrounded with danger because of your sins
And you're scared of more suffering to come.
Your sin has blinded you to the causes of your problem,
You're covered with problems because you won't repent.

Lord, may I not use my knowledge of You
As a club to beat someone into seeing things my way.
As Eliphaz who asked, *Isn't God in the heights of Heaven,*
Higher than the farthest star?
Job, don't say that's why God can't see you;
God can see through the blackness of the universe.
Job, you say the clouds block God's view and
El Shaddai just wanders around in Heaven
But God knows everything you do.
Are you going to keep believing in the old traditions,
The ones that deceive wicked people?
Those traditions didn't work for them,
They failed, and now the wicked are gone.
They said to God, 'Leave us alone.
El Shaddai can't do anything for us.'
Eliphaz said, *I can't see why the wicked said this,*
El Shaddai has filled their houses with good things.
When the righteous see the wicked destroyed
And the last of them burned up in fire,
They will laugh and rejoice.

Lord, help me to listen to the Holy Spirit's voice
And not be distracted by the bad advice
That people give me about Your will.
Eliphaz told Job, *Stop fussing with God,*
You will have peace when you yield to Him.
Listen to what the Spirit is saying to you
And He will prosper you again.
If you return to El Shaddai, He will receive you

And restore your life.

Quit lusting after riches,

>*And give away all the money you've horded.*

Then El Shaddai will be your reward

>*And you'll have more happiness than money can buy.*

El Shaddai will be your delight

>*And you'll be able to see God again.*

When you keep your vow and pray to God,

>*He will hear you and answer you.*

Your plans will be successful

>*And God will shine His light on your path.*

You will then realize why God has brought you low,

>*It was because of your past pride*

>*But you'll be saved if you'll be humble.*

If your hands are clean and your heart pure,

>*God will deliver you from this mess.*

Amen.

My Prayer

Lord, take away any blindness I have to my sin,

>*Keep me from being belligerent like Eliphaz.*

Help me to see my sin as You see it,

>*And I'll repent and seek Your forgiveness.*

Help me live a pure life.

Amen.

Chapters 23–24

JOB'S THIRD ANSWER TO ELIPHAZ

JOB tackles one of the most perplexing questions of all time, "Why is God hidden or silent?" Job wants God to tell him exactly why he is suffering. What Job doesn't know is that God has removed the "hedge" and has allowed satan to "try" him. God seemingly hides Himself because He wants us to trust Him in the darkness when we can't see His hand or hear His voice. We must practice in the darkness what we have learned in the light.

Lord, help me obey You when I can't hear Your voice
     And follow You when I can't see Your guiding hand.
  Job told Eliphaz, *I'm complaining like a bitter old person,*
     And groaning like a broken man.
  But I'm looking for God and can't find Him;
     I need to talk to Him about my troubles.
I would like to tell Him my side of the story,
     Then I'd listen to His explanation
     And understand why I'm suffering.
I don't think God would argue with me,
     He would pay attention to what I've got to say.
God would be fair and honest with me,
     We'd both know that it's not because of any sin.
Lord, help me find You when I search for answers
to my problems,
     As Job said when searching for You.
I search for God in the East, He's not there;
     I didn't find Him in the West.
I didn't find God when I searched in the North,
     And I still didn't see Him in the South.

Yet, God knows the way I take,
>*And when He has tried me in the fire*
>*I shall come out like purified gold.*
I have followed God's footsteps,
>*I didn't turn to the right or the left.*
I have not disobeyed the commands of His mouth,
>*But have guarded His words in my mouth.*
Lord, I yield my life to Your will,
>As Job recognized Your sovereignty in his life.
Job said, *No one can change God,*
>*And He does not change His mind;*
>*He accomplishes what He wants to do.*
So God controls my life,
>*He will do with me what He wills.*
When I think of God's awesome sovereignty,
>*I am terrified and worship Him.*
God, make my heart tender to do Your will;
>*I am afraid to disobey You.*
My suffering has imprisoned me,
>*I am surrounded by impenetrable gloom.*
>Amen.

My Prayer

Lord, I want the faith of Job
>*To trust You in dark sufferings,*
>*When I can't see my hand in front of my face.*
I yield my life to You, as did Job;
>*And just as Job worshiped You when he*
>*didn't know what to do,*
>*So I worship You.*
>*Amen.*

Chapter 24

QUESTIONS

Job asked, *Since God knows what'll happen every day,*
Why doesn't He tell those who know Him
What is going to happen each day?

Why doesn't God punish the wicked
Because they move the stakes that mark property?
The wicked rustle flocks and sell them for profit,
They steal welfare checks from the poor.
The wicked foreclose on the property of poor widows
And push away the needy.
The wicked force the hungry to scrounge for food
In garbage dumps or any place they can find it
So they have just enough for their family.

Lord, may I never mistreat poor people;
Job said, The poor work to make money
for their boss, but don't get a bonus or raise.
The poor don't have clothes to keep them warm,
They shiver in the storms and rain.
They try to get protection any way they can,
It's almost impossible to keep warm.

Lord, may I never be heartless as the wicked rich;
Job said of them, They mistreat orphans.
The wicked rich force the poor to hock their clothes
Before they will loan them any money
So the poor have to freeze in cold weather.
The wicked rich force the poor to serve their tables,

But won't give them any food.
The wicked rich make the poor work in their shops,
But won't give them fair wages for their work.
The poor everywhere are crying for help,
Yet God apparently does nothing about it.

Lord, I don't understand why evil people prosper;
Job said, Wicked people rebel against the light.
Evil people refuse to learn what is right,
They will not live by Your rules.
The murderer rises from his bed
To kill the innocent and needy,
When it's dark he becomes a thief.
The adulterer waits till no one sees him,
He doesn't want people to know what he does.
They commit their crimes under the cloak of darkness,
They sleep in the daytime.
None of them knows what is right or wrong,
They can't tell the difference between dark crimes,
And doing good things in the morning light.
They use people's fear of darkness
To cover their wickedness.

Lord, what is the future of evil people?
Job says, The wicked will disappear from the earth.
The wicked are scum who are washed away with the flood;
All they acquire is cursed.
The wicked will melt away
Just as heat melts the snow,
Hell will eat them up.
The wicked will be forgotten by his mother
And the worms of death will feed sweetly on him.
No one will remember the sinner,
They will be broken like a limb

Is snapped in a wind storm;
For they have taken advantage of the orphans,
And refused to help widows.

Lord, help me to see life through Your eyes,
As Job understood Your justice.
Job said, *God puts down the wicked*
Even if they rise for a short time.
God allows the wicked to live for a time
But He constantly watches their actions.
Though the wicked may be momentarily powerful,
They're gone in the twinkle of an eye.
They are gathered in death like everyone else,
Then their bodies shrivel up and die.
Job challenged his three counselors, *Tell me if I'm wrong;*
No one can prove otherwise.
Amen.

My Prayer

Lord, it's so obvious that wicked people prosper on this earth
Even when they rebel against Your principles.
Don't let me be blinded by money and power;
I know You will punish the wicked
At the Great White Judgment throne.
Help me live by Your godly principles during my time on earth.
Amen.

Chapter 25

BILDAD'S THIRD RESPONSE

BILDAD has nothing new to say to Job, he just repeats what has already been said by the other counselors which is: "God is sovereign and man is nothing,"

Lord, help me understand the truth of Your sovereignty,
> And yield to Your purpose in my life.
Bildad said, *God has all power and dominion,*
> *He rules in high places;*
> *Men should fear Him.*
God has more armies than anyone can number,
> *And He gives light to all on the earth.*
How can you, Job, possibly stand before God
> *And claim to be righteous?*
> *No one on earth is pure.*
Even the moon that shines at night
> *Or the sparkling stars are not pure.*
How can you claim to be pure,
> *You're just a worm in God's sight.*
> Amen.

My Prayer

Lord, I know I'm a sinner
> *And I'm not perfect.*
But I am grateful the blood of Jesus Christ Your Son
> *Cleanses me from all sin (1 John 1:7).*

I stand perfect in Your presence
Because Jesus has taken away my sin.
Amen.

Chapter 26

JOB'S RESPONSE TO BILDAD

JOB sarcastically suggests God will be God without Bildad's help, God doesn't need someone to defend Him. Then Job displays in this chapter an impressive understanding of God's majesty and power. Finally, Job ends by stating that no one can fully understand what God is doing in the world (Job 2:14).

Lord, may I know how to answer bad advice
        As Job told Bildad, *You haven't done anything.*
    You haven't given help to the helpless,
        Nor rescued a person who was lost.
    You give me un-needed advice,
        You haven't said anything that makes sense.
    Where did you get all these ideas?
        Are you repeating what you've heard from others?

Lord, may I have great understanding of Your greatness
        As Job who declared, *The dead tremble before You;*
        Even Hell can't hide from You.
    God hangs the earth on nothing,
        And spreads the northern sky in empty space.
    God fills the thick clouds with rain,

And they do not burst with its weight.

God covers His throne so no one can see it,

> *No one can see God and live.*

God fixed a boundary between light and darkness,

> *He determined the oceans would not flood dry land.*

By His power, God stirs up the seas with a storm,

> *And by His skill He stills the face of the waters.*

By God's Spirit, He makes the heavens beautiful,

> *And His power restrains the slithering serpent.*

We see only the edges of His power,

> *And we hear only a whisper of His voice.*

When His power thunders across the land,

> *Who can fully know His greatness?*

> Amen.

My Prayer

Lord, I see so many reflections of You in this world,

> *Yet, there is so much more to discover.*

Help me understand Your purpose for my life,

> *And help me learn of You in Your Word.*

> *Amen.*

Chapter 27

JOB MAINTAINS HIS INTEGRITY

IN Chapter 26 Job asks his three comforters if they have had any success in counseling others. None of them answer, so Job again proclaims his innocence. Job seems to say, "Yes, I agree that the wicked will be punished, but if anyone needs to be reminded of this, you three need it; not me."

Lord, I will maintain my integrity
    As did Job who took an oath,
I swear by the Living God
    Who has taken away my rights,
And I vow by El Shaddai
    Who has dealt bitterly with me,
That as long as I live and as long as I have breath
    I will not curse or speak evil
    Nor will I tell a lie. So,
I can't say what you three want me to say;
    That would be telling a lie.
I will not disobey my conscience,
    I will keep my integrity till I die.
Lord, I want to be faithful to You as Job
    Who was always true to You.
Job said, *May you three be like the wicked*
    Who will suffer the fate of the unrighteous.
What hope will you hypocrites have
    When God takes away your life?
Will God hear the cry of the wicked?
    Will God help them when trouble comes?

The problem with the wicked,
They will not call upon El Shaddai;
They will not turn to God.

Lord, teach me the ways You work with the wicked,
I want to know what You will do.

What will the wicked receive from El Shaddai?
The unrighteous will be judged by Him.
If the wicked are rewarded with many children,
They will still die by starvation or illness;
No one will grieve them.
If the wicked have lots of money, and clothes,
Someone else will spend their money and wear their clothes.
If the wicked build a large mansion,
It will collapse like their evil reputation.
The wicked will go to bed rich,
But all their wealth is gone when he wakes up."
The wicked are fearful of everything all the time,
They can't sleep at night for worry.
The Eastern sandstorm blows everything away,
They are battered by the storms of life.
The hurricanes pound them without mercy,
The wicked only struggle to survive;
What kind of life is that?
Amen.

My Prayer

Lord, I know that You will judge the wicked,
So keep me from ignorant sins;
Or even worse, from rebellious sins.
Keep me pure of motives and separate from sin.
Amen.

Chapter 28

JOB DISCUSSES WISDOM

THIS chapter is about the wisdom of God. In verses 1-11 Job describes various precious metals and stones, but declares wisdom is more valuable than them all. So, *"where can wisdom be found"* (Job 28:12)? The answer, *"Behold, the fear of the Lord, that is wisdom, and to depart from evil is understanding"* (Job 28:28).

Lord, I want Your wisdom more than anything in life,
>   And give me understanding to use it properly.
Job said, *Silver is found in the deep mines,*
>   *And gold is hidden in veins within the earth.*
Iron must be dug from the earth,
>   *And copper must be smelted from rocks.*
Miners must use light to dig in dark caverns,
>   *So they can dig ever deeper for earth's treasures.*
They break open new shafts in the earth.
>   *Yet those walking on the earth's surface*
>   *Don't know what's beneath them;*
Just as people in this life
>   *Don't realize the valuable things about them.*

The ground above grows bread to eat,
>   *The earth below is mined into precious metals.*
Men have learned how to find sapphires,
>   *And how to dig gold out of the ground.*
No high flying falcon can see these precious things,
>   *No birds of prey can dig them up.*
No wild beast can unearth them,
>   *The lion does not know their value.*

People can crush the rocks to find sapphires,
      They can overturn mountains to find valuable things.
They can cut ditches to discover precious stones,
      And dam up streams to unearth precious treasures.
But they do not know where to find wisdom,
      And they can't unearth understanding.
No one realizes the value of wisdom,
      It can't be found anywhere in the earth.

The heart of the earth says,
      'Wisdom is not here,'
      The depth of the sea says,
      'Wisdom is not here!'
No one can buy wisdom with gold,
      And there's not enough silver to purchase it.
There's not enough gold in the richest mine
      To trade for wisdom,
      Neither can onyx or sapphires get it.
There is no comparison of wisdom to gold;
      A chest of gold could not substitute for it,
      Let alone crystal or any other valuable thing.
The price of wisdom is far above rubies,
      Not to mention coral or quartz.
The topaz of Ethiopia is not its equal,
      Wisdom is the most valuable thing on earth.

Lord, give me wisdom to know all things,
      And give me understanding to use it properly.
Job asks, *Where does wisdom come from?*
      What is the source of understanding?
Inasmuch as the birds of the sky can't see it,
      It—like jewels and precious metals—is hidden from the eye.
Only when one dies and it's too late,
      Do people understand the truth of wisdom.

God alone understands the value of wisdom,
  He manifests it throughout the earth.
God who determines the direction and power of the wind,
  Also puts the oceans and rivers in their place.
God who made laws for the rain,
  Also determines when lightning shall strike.
God who did all this knows
  That wisdom is the most important thing in the world.
God established everything on earth by wisdom,
  And He tells everyone on earth about its value.
To obey the Lord is the wisest thing in life,
  And those with understanding run from evil.
        Amen.

My Prayer

Lord, I want to be wiser than I am.
  Take away any blindness I have.
Reveal Your plan to me for my life;
  Help me see truth and do it.
        Amen.

Chapter 29

JOB'S NOSTALGIC SOLILOQUY

IN this chapter Job describes his past prosperity and former happiness, while in the next chapter he bewails his present suffering. Many writers call this chapter Job's *soliloquy*—to talk to oneself in dramatic monologue.

Lord, help me look back on my past life,
> And praise You for Your sovereign leadership.
Job reflected, *I remember the past days in my life*
> *When God watched over me,*
When I had God's light shining on my path,
> *And I walked easily through the dark night.*
I remember when I was young
> *And I felt the presence of God in my life.*
I remember El Shaddai guiding my decisions,
> *And I had all my children around me.*
My businesses prospered,
> *And everything went well.*
I went to places where important people gathered,
> *And they considered me one of them.*
The young people respected me,
> *And the aged were glad to see me.*
The city officials would listen to me,
> *And they wanted to know my opinions.*
Those who heard me, listened to my thoughts,
> *Everyone spoke well of me*
Because I gave to the poor who asked for help,
> *And I gave to orphans when no one else would do it.*

I gave help to those about to die,
> *And widows were appreciative of my assistance.*
I did the right thing and people called me righteous,
> *My reputation was like a robe and crown.*
I was eyes for the blind,
> *And feet for the lame.*
I was a father for the needy,
> *And made sure that everything was done right.*
I broke the fangs of the wicked,
> *And took victims from their mouth.*
I thought I would die comfortably in my own bed
> *Surrounded by loving family and friends.*
I was like a spreading fruitful tree
> *Whose branches were refreshed by the rain.*
I was constantly renewed,
> *And I kept getting more power.*
People listened to me for my wisdom,
> *They didn't say anything against my opinion.*
My words were like the rain
> *That refreshed everyone who heard me.*
I encouraged all those who were discouraged,
> *And my optimism lifted them up.*
I could tell people how to live,
> *And they listened to me;*
> *I comforted the mourners.*

Amen.

My Prayer

Lord, Job looked back on all the good things he had in life.
> *I, too, look back and praise You for every good thing that has happened to me.*

I know that every good thing comes from You.
Thank You for them all.
Amen.

❧━┼┼━❧

Chapter 30

JOB DESCRIBES HIS PATHETIC CONDITION

IN the previous chapter, Job reviewed his past blessings, but in this chapter he contrasts his pathetic state. Job not only is suffering, but he feels mental and emotional alienation. The downtrodden he previously helped now rejects him. Job's former wealthy friends scorn him. All who previously respected Job now turn their backs on him, even his wife has abandoned him. But in spite of every downturn, Job lifts his head to reaffirm his integrity before God.

Lord, I feel pain for Job,
> Give me sympathetic friends when I go through suffering.
Job lamented, *I am now mocked by young men,*
> *Those thugs who are the lowest in society.*
They have attacked and hurt me,
> *Their assaults do me no good;*
> *They have done nothing to help me.*
Their ethical character has gone,
> *They are devoid of spiritual appetite.*
They gnaw in the dirt for a depraved bone,
> *There is no integrity in any of them.*
They live in holes in the ground or among the rocks,
> *They hide in the bushes like animals.*

They are foolish nobodies
  Completely empty of human virtues.

Lord, I understand why Job rejected his ungrateful critics,
      Especially after he had done so much for them.
  Job said, *Now they taunt me,*
      They even use my name as a curse word.
  They won't come near me
      Except to spit in my face.
  Because God has allowed these troubles to afflict me,
      They have rejected me and hate me.
  These wretched people attack me,
      They trip me up so I fall helplessly on my face.
  They block my way so I can't get through,
      They laugh at me in public places,
      Knowing I can't help myself.
  They attack me from the front and behind,
      And kick me when I fall down.

I am scared of them
      Because I can't defend myself.
  My honor has gone,
      Blown away by a strong wind.
  Now I'm a broken old man,
      Because of my desperate condition
      And no one helps me.
  I can't sleep because of my pain,
      Like something eating on my bones.
  My clothes stink and are stained with my sores,
      My coat hangs on me because I've lost so much weight.
  God has thrown me into this hog pen,
      I've sunk into the mud and mire.

Lord, give me sympathy for Job, and for all others
      Who are suffering from debilitating pain.

Job cried, *God, I need You,*
> *But You do not answer me.*
God, I stand before You,
> *But You do not see me.*
Why are You cruel to me?
> *Your powerful hand is persecuting me.*
I'm tossed to and fro by every wind,
> *I don't know where I'm going.*
The only thing I know for sure is that
> *I'll die just as every person must die. Surely,*
God, You would not punish
> *A man who is already ruined!*
If a man cried for mercy,
> *I know You, God, wouldn't destroy him.*

Have I not wept for those in trouble?
> *Was not my soul grieved for the poor?*
Yet, when I looked for something good,
> *All I got was bad treatment.*
When I expected light,
> *Darkness came and everything was black.*
My mind is all confused, and I don't understand
> *Why am I suffering all this misery?*
I look for the sunshine, but get gloom;
> *I cry for help, but no one answers.*
Instead, people consider me crazy like a hyena,
> *Or I've stuck my head in the sand like an ostrich.*
My flesh is black with infection,
> *My skin rots and falls off,*
> *And I'm burning up with a fever.*
My harp only plays mournful tunes,
> *And my flute accompanies my weeping.*

Amen.

My Prayer

Lord, I understand why Job is bitter;
> *Help me keep my courage when things get dark for me,*
> *As they did for Job.*
Help me rejoice in sufferings as did Paul who said,
"I know how to be abased, and I know how to abound.
Everywhere and in all things I have learned both to be full and
to be hungry, both to abound and to suffer need"
(Phil. 4:12).
> > *Amen.*

Chapter 31

JOB'S FINAL PLEA OF INNOCENCE

Lord, help me know when I do right and what I do wrong,
> Don't let me be a hypocrite.
> *Job stated, God has given to each one of us a choice,*
> > *It comes with His gift of life to us.*
> *God will destroy those who work iniquity,*
> > *And He rewards those who obey Him in integrity.*
> *I made a vow to have integrity before God;*
> > *That vow includes not lusting after a woman,*
> > *And I have kept that vow.*
> *I have not been a hypocrite or lied to anyone,*

100

I have kept my word and done my duty.
I have always paid my debts,
　　And kept honest books before God.
If I didn't walk a straight path,
　　But turned to the left or to the right,
　　May I lose everything I gained.

If I have given into the enticement of women
　　Or lustfully flirted with another man's wife,
May I lose my family and be humiliated:
　　For sexual sin is a crime that should be punished.
Sexual lust burns like a devastating forest fire,
　　Devouring everything it touches.

I have not mistreated my servants,
　　And I carefully listened to their complaints.
How could I face God who created masters and servants,
　　If I did not treat them fairly?
I have not refused to give help to the poor,
　　Nor have I crushed the expectation of widows who need help;
　　I have always given to orphans and widows.
I have given clothes to the homeless who were naked,
　　And they have always thanked me
　　For keeping them warm and protected.
If I have ever hit an orphan or the poor,
　　Let my arm fall off in judgment.
That would be better than letting God judge me,
　　Because I can't endure His punishment.

Making money has never been my life's passion,
　　Nor have I placed my confidence in my checkbook.
My life is not based on my wealth,
　　Nor is my happiness dependent on riches and possessions.

I have never been enticed to worship idols, nor have I done so;
    I have admired the setting sun and bright morning,
    But never have I thought of making an idol of them.
Anyone worshiping idols deserves judgment from God,
    For they would have denied God who created them.

I have never rejoiced when my enemies failed,
    Nor was I glad when they were punished.
I would have sinned with my mouth,
    If I cursed those who hate me.
My servants have never turned away the hungry,
    And I have opened my doors to travelers.
I have not tried to cover my sins
    As most people do.
I realize sin can't be covered or ignored;
    Everyone eventually will find out,
    And I would be ashamed to show my face in public.

If only there was someone who would listen,
    And not judge me before learning the facts.
If only El Shaddai would show me my sins,
    Or someone prove in a court of law
    That I have broken the moral law.
Even if my financial record shows I've stolen,
    Or, they find stolen goods in my possession,
    Or, they find a dead body that I've murdered,
Then, I would admit that I have sinned;
    I wouldn't deny it!

Then, let me be judged according to my sins,
    And let me be punished according to my crime.
But, I stand by my actions and my testimony,
    I have integrity with God.
                    Amen.

My Prayer

Lord, I want the integrity of Job.
I want to be able to stand blameless among people,
Knowing I have not sinned against them.
And if I have sinned against any—show me what I've done—
I'll go to them and ask forgiveness.
Forgive my trespasses as I forgive those who trespass against me.
Amen.

Chapter 32

ELIHU'S RESPONSE

Elihu: The Last Counselor

Job's three counselors refused to say any more to Job
    because he kept maintaining his integrity.
Then young Elihu became very angry at Job
    because he kept maintaining he was innocent,
        and because Job felt God was wrong for punishing him.
Elihu was also angry with the three counselors,
    Because they hadn't proven their point,
        but they unjustly condemned Job anyway.
Elihu had waited until the three quit speaking

because of their advanced age,
then he was ready to speak.

Elihu is the youngest comforter to visit Job. Elihu has the characteristics of youth; he is egotistical, very sure of what he's saying and has an inordinate opinion of himself. Elihu is argumentative and emotional.

Elihu reviews what the three comforters were saying. He agrees with their condemnation of Job (Job 34:34-37) although he thinks he gives a better presentation because of their inconclusive results (Job 32:2-5).

Elihu believes affliction at the hand of God is good. He describes how God speaks through dreams and visions, and the need of a friend (himself) to interpret them (Job 33:13-28). He tries to set himself up as Job's mediator (Job 33:5-7), yet his remarks about God's power and wisdom are filled with self-importance.

The name Elihu means "He is my God." He has a biblical name because he is a distant relative of Job's. Elihu is from the same family as Abraham. Elihu is a descendent of Buz, a son of Abraham's grandfather (Job 32:2; Gen. 12:24; Gen. 22:21). Elihu has come the longest distance from the Euphrates River region, the same area from which Abraham came.

Like a young man when he runs out of content, Elihu begins to ramble. His words become disjointed and incoherent. Then God cuts Elihu off with the sarcastic observation, *"Who is this who darkens counsel by words without knowledge"* (Job 38:2)?

Elihu, a distant relative told the three, I am young,
> *And you're too old to understand the problem.*
So I held back until you were finished,
> *I didn't dare express my opinion before now.*
I thought, Age should speak first
> *Because the aged has more wisdom.*
But wisdom comes from the spirit of a man,
> *Wisdom comes from the breath of El Shaddai.*
Therefore, the elders are not automatically wise,

And no one automatically gets smart
    By living a long time.
As a result, listen to me—because I know the answer,
    I will now tell you the truth.

I have patiently listened to your words,
        And tried to follow your arguments
        As you were searching for the right words.
I paid careful attention to all three of you,
        But none of you refuted Job's reasoning;
        You lost the argument.
Don't tell me Job is too smart for you,
        And only God can defeat Job.
If I had been arguing against Job
        I wouldn't have used your weak rebuttals.
You sat there in defeat with no response,
        And you didn't have anything else to say.
Must I remain silent because you lost the argument?
        No! I will tell you what I think.
I understand Job's problem,
        And I can explain the answer to all.
I feel like a barrel that's about to explode;
        I have to speak before I burst.
I've got to tell you what's on my mind
        To get any relief for myself.
I won't flatter anyone with what I'll say,
        And I'll show no favor to any.
If I did play favorites—and not speak the truth—
        My Creator would soon push me aside.
                Amen.

My Prayer

Lord, when I hear the arrogance of Elihu,
I am convicted by the pride of my heart.
Forgive me of boasting and presumptuousness,
Keep me from being important in my own eyes.
Take away my vanity and give me a spirit of humility.
Amen.

Chapter 33

ELIHU'S CHARGE AGAINST JOB

Elihu's Problem

WHAT Elihu says about God in this chapter is right, but what he says about Job is wrong. Elihu commits the sin of a young man, he talked before he listened. Elihu judged Job before he listened to him.

Elihu said to Job,

Listen to what I am going to say,
And do what I tell you to do.
The truth is on the tip of my tongue,
My words come from a sincere heart.
The spirit of God has made me,
The breath of El Shaddai gives me life.

See if you can answer me and
  Express your thoughts in logical order.
You and I are the same before God,
  We are both molded from clay;
  But I will be your spokesman to God.
You don't need to be afraid of me,
  I will treat you right.

Lord, help me know who is telling me the truth,
  So I can trust them in my hour of need.
Elihu said to Job, *I was previously listening to you,*
  And I heard what you said.
You said you were pure, without transgression,
  You maintained your integrity.
You claimed God was punishing you,
  And had made you His enemy,
  That God had made you His prisoner.

Elihu told Job, *You are wrong in your opinion,*
  Let me show you where.
You, Job, said, 'God is greater than any person
  So why do you fight God?'
God does not need to defend Himself;
  God has spoken once, sometimes twice
  Yet, you still miss the point.

Elihu explained, *God speaks to the minds of people*
  When they are asleep.
God speaks in a dream or a vision at night,
  When a person is sleeping deeply;
  God warns them of their actions.
God wants people to change their mind,
  So they won't be proud and rebellious.
God warns so they won't die,
  Or so they won't go to hell.

Lord, may I listen to my conscience
  As Elihu wanted Job to obey his conscience.
Elihu told Job, *God also warns with pain*
  So that the body suffers continually
  And they waste away to skin and bones.
They stand at the doorway to death,
  Ready to be cast into hell;
  Job, is this your problem?

Before God, you will need an intercessor
  Who can vouch for your integrity,
Who will plead for God to be gracious to you,
  Because the intercessor has paid a ransom for you,
  And will redeem you from being cast into hell.

When your body is then redeemed by God,
  Your flesh will be as youthful as a child's.
You will pray and God will hear you,
  You will see God's face,
  And God will reward your faithfulness.
But you must declare before everyone,
  'I have sinned before God;
  I deserve my punishment.'
Yes, God redeems those heading to Hell,
  God can fill their life with light.
God can accomplish all these things for you,
  He'll do it twice, even three times,
To bring you back from the edge of Hell
  So you can live in the light.

Job, pay attention to what I am saying,
  Keep quiet and don't interrupt me.
So if you will acknowledge your sin,
  Speak, because I want to hear it from your lips.
If not, then keep quiet;

Listen to me and I'll tell you the truth.
Amen.

My Prayer

Lord, Elihu was right in what he knew about You,
But he was wrong about Job.
Help me to always listen to You so I can know You better.
Amen.

Chapter 34

ELIHU TELLS OF GOD'S JUSTICE

Then Elihu said to Job and the three counselors,
> *Listen to me, you aged men of wisdom;*
> *You don't know as much as you think you do.*
Just as the ear knows good music,
> *And the mouth knows good food,*
> *Let us choose what is good in my words.*
Job says, 'I am righteous
> *But God is not treating me fairly.'*
Job thinks people accuse him of hiding his sin
> *Because he still suffers under God.*
Has there ever lived a man as stubborn as Job
> *Who denies the truth of his suffering?*
Job probably has evil friends,

And he probably parties with lawbreakers.
Didn't Job arrogantly say
It's impossible to please God?

Listen to what I think,
You'll agree with me if you have understanding.
God cannot sin, nor can El Shaddai do evil;
He punishes people when they sin,
And He rewards people who do the right thing.
Job, it's obvious you'd sinned
Because God is judging your life;
If you did good, God would reward you.
Read my lips, 'God will not do wrong,
The Almighty will always reward righteousness.'
Everyone would perish if God judged sin;
If God took back the Spirit He gave us,
No one would live.

If you have understanding, Job, listen to me;
Could God control the world if He did not punish sin?
You make God look foolish by saying,
'I am righteous but I'm also suffering.'

Kings who are wicked and unjust
Will not cause a righteous man to suffer.
God punishes the lawbreakers
Whether they are rich or poor;
God treats them all alike.
All were created by God, and at death's house,
They all pass away and are removed from this life.

God's eyes see all that people do,
Nothing they do escapes God's watch.
There is no darkness in death
Where the unrighteous can hide themselves;

No darkness is thick enough to hide from God.
No one has any warning when death comes,
And they appear before God for judgment.
God allows the mighty to be destroyed,
And places another person in their place.
God knows everything they do,
And in one night they lose everything they have.
God openly judges the sin of the sinner,
So all can learn from what happened.
God judges them openly because they
Have turned aside from following Him.
God judges the mighty because He has ignored
The cries of the poor and oppressed them.

But if God was absent, and hid His face,
We could blame Him with the trouble
We see on earth.
Just as when an evil person becomes ruler,
We could blame Him for our suffering.
But God sees all we do,
He punishes all our sin.
So you Job, are punished because of sin;
God has not hid His face from judgment.

No one can ever say to God,
'You have chastened me but I haven't sinned.'
Nor have they said to God, 'I will stop sinning
If you tell me what to do.'

Must God punish according to your standards?
The answer is 'No!'
But, Job, you think your standards are God's standards.
Wise people will say you—Job—are not thinking clearly,
Intelligent people will agree with me.

Job you will be on trial for a long time
>*Because your answers come from your wicked heart.*
You have added rebellion to your sin,
>*And now you are blaspheming God.*
>>*Amen.*

❦═╪ ╪═❦

My Prayer

Lord, I know You see all I do, and You hear all I say,
>*And You know all I think.*
Forgive me of any secret sin,
>*And I need Your grace because I am not perfect.*
Give me Your strength to do better in all of my life.
>*May I continually please You in thought, word and deed.*
>>*Amen.*

❦═╪ ╪═❦

Chapter 35

ELIHU'S QUESTIONS

ELIHU pauses at the beginning of this chapter to see if Job or the three counselors would answer him. They don't, so Elihu speaks directly to Job. He begins with three questions: (1) Why live a righteous life? (2) Does your sin hurt God? (3) How do the good things you do help God?

Elihu tried to point out Job's inconsistencies,
 "First you claim you are righteous before God,
Then you say living a righteous life has no benefits;
 Let me ask you three questions."
'What's the use of living a righteous life?'"
 Elihu told Job, 'Is God pleased?'"
"If you sin, how does it hurt God?
 If you sin many times
 How will it affect God?"
"If you do good, how does it help God?
 Could your goodness
 Possibly contribute anything to God?"

"No! Your sins hurt only yourself,
 And your good works only help other people."
"The oppressed suffer from tribulations,
 They mourn under those with power."
"Yet, they never cry out for God, their Creator
 Who gives songs in the night."
"The oppressed never ask, 'Where is the Creator
 Who makes us smarter than birds and animals?'"
"When a person cries out to God,
 The Lord does not answer that one person
Because that one finite person would think
 He alone could get God's attention."
"Yet, God does listen to what we say;
 El Shaddai is concerned about our problems."
"And further, God sees what happens down here,
 And He will judge all evil in this world
 But you must wait for His time."
"Job, do not complain to God
 Because He does not get angry,
 As you have gotten angry."
"You have made yourself look foolish

By protesting because you're suffering."
Amen

My Prayer

Lord, keep me from criticism when I should be quiet.
Help me accept things in life I don't understand,
Especially when I don't know all the facts.
Give me a quiet heart in Your presence.
Amen.

Chapters 36–37

ELIHU CLAIMS TO SPEAK FOR GOD

ELIHU pauses to see if Job or the three counselors have anything to say. Again, silence. So Elihu continues speaking, claiming to speak for God.

Elihu asked Job, *Bear with me,*
I still have words to speak on God's behalf.
I have learned from many sources
About the way the Creator does things right.
I am not stretching the truth,
My knowledge about God is true.
God is almighty in knowledge and power,
So He does not despise anyone.

He does not let the wicked get away with their sins,
And the oppressed will eventually get justice.
He sees every thing the righteous do,
And rewards rulers who do things right.
When trouble comes upon the righteous
and they suffer affliction,
God lets them know why they are oppressed.
God shows them their sin when they misbehave,
He uses suffering to get their attention
So they will repent and turn from evil.
Job, why can't you see your condition?
God is punishing you because of sin.

Those who listen and obey God are blessed by Him,
God prospers them throughout their life.
If they refuse to listen to God,
They will die violently before their time,
And they won't realize it's because of their sin.
The evil person hates God, they won't ask for mercy;
Even when God punished them for sin,
They die prematurely because of their wasted life.
But God gets the attention of sinners through suffering,
And their affliction turns them around.

And now Job, your wickedness has corrupted your thinking;
You have refused to acknowledge the punishment of God.
God would have brought you out of this distress,
And given you a table full of delicious food,
But you have refused to repent.
The wrath of God is coming shortly,
And when it does, it will fall on you
Because when God punishes the unrighteous,
There is no way you can escape it.

Job, you have wrongly claimed to be righteous,
> *Because God blessed you with wealth and position.*
Don't pray for the night to come,
> *Because that's when most people die.*
Don't turn to evil because you feel cut off,
> *For God originally sent you suffering*
> *To keep you from evil. Remember,*
God has all power,
> *No one can teach lessons like God.*
No one can tell God what to do,
> *No one can tell God He made a mistake.*

Always sing the praises of God,
> *Magnify His works in the world.*
I'm telling you things that everyone knows,
> *But no one knows the way of God completely.*
God is exalted greater than our understanding,
> *No one can number His years.*

God draws water into the clouds,
> *Then He distills it into rain that falls from Heaven*
> *And benefits all below.*
Can anyone understand how
the clouds spread out over Heaven,
> *Or how thunder rolls over the earth,*
> *Or how it replenishes the ocean depths?*
By these mighty demonstrations of power,
> *God provides abundant food for us to eat.*
His hand is evident in the crashing thunder,
> *The storm demonstrates His power to judge.*
>> Amen.

My Prayer

Lord, I believe You have power to do anything You desire.
I see Your awesome power in all the world about me.
Because of Your sovereignty and omnipotence,
I will live righteously.
Because of Your love for me, I will live godly.
Amen.

Chapter 37

ELIHU CONTINUES

Elihu continued his speech,
The power of God thrills my heart,
And I jump for joy.
Listen, you'll hear God speaking through thunder,
It rumbles from His mouth across the valleys.
God's thunder is heard every place under Heaven,
His lightning spreads out over the whole earth.
Next comes the echo of the thunder,
It returns as a roaring voice,
And God does not hold back its volume.
God's voice is glorious and majestic,
We humans cannot fathom the greatness of His power.

God tells the snow to fall in the winter upon the earth,
>   In the spring he directs both the gentle and heavy rain.
Then everyone stops working till the rain is over,
>   They watch God's power with amazement.
When winter comes, animals go into their dens
>   And remain there for the season.
Storms come from the south,
>   Biting winter winds come from the north.
God blows upon the ponds of water,
>   And they freeze, turning to ice.
The clouds roll and swirl in the air,
>   They go where God commands.
God causes things to happen on earth
>   Either to correct His people,
>   Or to bless them with His mercy.

Job, you need to listen to me,
>   Think about all the works of God.
Can you control the storms like God?
>   Can you bring lightning flashing from the clouds?
Can you place the clouds in the sky like God?
>   Don't you know that God has perfect knowledge and power?
Can you bring the sweltering heat from the sky,
>   So that your clothes are wet with perspiration?
Can you make the cooling wind die down,
>   So that people are baked by the sun,
>   Like a giant fire that burns the skin?
Job, you think you are so smart,
>   Tell us what to say to God;
>   Are we left in the darkness?
Job, tell God we want to speak to Him;
>   Don't let God eat us up alive.

We cannot look into the face of God,
  Just as we cannot look into the bright sun
  When there's not a cloud in the sky.
Golden splendor comes from God's presence,
  He is surrounded with awesome majesty.
We cannot begin to conceive His majesty,
  Yet in His power, God doesn't squash us;

And in His mercy God doesn't oppress us
  (As you, Job, think God oppresses you).
Therefore, people everywhere fear God;
  Wise people will honor Him.
     Amen.

My Prayer

Lord, You are great in power and wisdom.
  You created the huge things in this universe
  And I stand in awe of Your power.
  Your wisdom created the complexities of human beings
  and I praise You for how I am created.
    Your beauty is seen in the design of this universe.
I worship You.
     Amen.

Chapters 38—40:2

GOD CHALLENGES JOB WITH HIS POWER

GOD spoke directly to Job, not to Elihu or the three counselors, although they probably heard what Job heard. None actually saw God, for He is a Spirit, and *"there shall no man see Me, and live"* (Exod. 33:20). They saw only a storm (*whirlwind*, Job 38:1, KJV) just as another place some saw only fire, *"And the LORD spoke to you out of the midst of the fire. You heard the sound of the words, but saw no form; [you] only [heard] a voice"* (Deut. 4:12).

God rebukes Elihu for speaking out of his ignorance. When God says, "Stand up," He tells them, "Get ready, I'm coming, ready or not."

The remainder of Chapters 38-39 reveals the majesty and mystery of God. Only a wise omnipotent God could create an awesomely powerful universe, and only an all-knowing God could weave all the intricate parts of the universe into a beautiful coherent pattern. In contrast, man is limited, weak, and finite. Compared to God, man can't do anything, and man knows nothing. This is God's way of explaining to Job and his comforters that they can't explain the reason for pain, the source of goodness, or the purpose of life. Man is completely finite in God's presence, all he can do is listen and worship.

The Lord answered Job out of the storm,
> *Who is this Elihu who speaks out of ignorance*
> *To question My way of doing things?*
> *Stand up like a man to take My criticism,*
> *I will ask the questions*
> *And you must answer Me.*
> *Where were you when I created the earth?*
> *You must answer that question*

Since you think you're so smart.
Do you know who determined how big the earth would be,
    And who drew its design?
Do you know who laid the earth's foundation,
    Or who laid the cornerstone?
The angels were watching
        From the first row of Heaven,
        Applauding and singing for joy.

Can you command a new morning to dawn,
        And give to the world a new day,
So that the wickedness done at night
        Is brought to an end?
Can you make the red sun rise
        To shine its golden rays to all,
So that light dispels wickedness,
        And stops acts of violence?

Do you know the source of the waters of the sea,
        Have you explored the depths of the oceans?
Do you know the location of the doors of death,
        Or can you find the gates to Hell?
Do you understand everything about the earth?
        Tell Me if you know it all.

Do you know where light comes from?
        Where does darkness go where there is no light?
Can you lead someone to the home of light?
        Do you know where to find it?
Do you know all these answers?
        Were you living when I created everything?
Are you old enough to know all things?

Have you gone to snow houses to get snow?
        Do you know where to find hail?

I keep the snow and hail to send
    In a time of trouble,
      To carry out My purpose in the world.

Where does light come from?
    And where is the east wind when it's not blowing?
Who cuts the channels where rivers flow,
    And who controls where lightning strikes?
Who makes rain fall in the barren desert
    Where no one lives,
Soaking the dry desolate earth
    Until grass sprouts out of the ground?
Does the rain have a father,
    Or does the dew have a mother?
Who gives birth to the frost that falls around you,
    And ice that becomes hard as stone,
    And who freezes solid the surfaces of water?

Can you tie the stars into a cluster,
    Or hold back Pleiades and Orion?
Can you make sure the seasons come in proper order,
    Or guide the stars across the sky?
Do you know the laws of the heavens
    That control the universe,
    So that it properly influences the earth?

Can you yell loud enough to make it rain?
    Will the lightning go where you command it to strike?
Who created people with the capacity to know things,
    And gave them the ability to understand things?
Can you count the number of all the clouds?
    Can you tilt over the water jugs of Heaven
    To turn dust into mud?
Can you provide food for the lioness
    To feed her young lion's hunger?

Can you provide food for the ravens
> *To give to their young hungry children?*
Amen.

Chapter 39

GOD CONTINUES

Do you know why the ostrich flaps its wings?
> *It can't fly like the stork.*
She lays her eggs in the sand
> *For the warm ground to hatch them.*
She doesn't realize a foot could crush them,
> *Or a wild animal could destroy them.*
The ostrich treats its young heartlessly,
> *As though they were not her own.*
She doesn't worry about those things;
> *Once she lays her eggs, she goes her way.*
I have not given wisdom to the ostrich,
> *It is devoid of understanding.*
But when she gets up to run,
> *She is faster than a horse with a rider.*
Did you give the horse its strength,
> *And did you clothe its neck with a mane?*
Did you create the horse to leap like a locust,
> *Isn't its snorting majestic?*
The horse paws the ground to show off its strength,
> *Then it charges unafraid into battle,*

Not fearing imminent danger.
When arrows fly in the heat of battle,
And swords slash around it,
The horse rushes fiercely into danger.
When the trumpet sounds to attack,
The horse senses the battle is on,
And charges toward the enemy.

Were you wise enough to create a hawk
That spreads its wings,
And soars in the sky?
Can you command the eagle to fly into the heavens,
And build its nest in the heights?
It lives on the rocky crag,
From there it spots its prey afar off.
The eagle brings back the spoils of war
To feed its young.

Amen.

Chapter 40

THE LORD SPEAKS

Moreover, the Lord said to Job,
Do you still want to debate with Me?
Those who argue with El Shaddai
Must still answer to Him.

Amen.

My Prayer

Lord, I am amazed at the greatness of Your power,
And Your wisdom in creating the universe.
There are so many things I have never thought about,
But You have a reason for everything;
You have a plan for this universe.
I worship You for Your awesome greatness,
And for Your brilliant wisdom;
I accept Your plan for my life.
Amen.

Chapter 40:3–5

JOB RESPONDS TO THE LORD IN REPENTANCE

LOOK at Job's brief humble response to God in this short section. What a great contradiction to Job's earlier self-confident challenge to God. Job had wanted to meet God in a court of law to defend his integrity. Job had bragged about his ability to present his case (Job 23:1-2). But now Job puts his hand over his mouth and apologizes for speaking too much.

What changed Job? God asked 49 questions to demonstrate His sovereignty and lordship over all creation, including God's mastery of Job himself. This barrage of questions is like a courtroom cross-examination where the defendant—Job—withers under divine interrogation.

Now Job is completely silent. He can only acknowledge his vileness (Job 40:4).

God continues with questions in Chapters 40 and 41 and at last (Job 42:1-6), Job repents in dust and ashes (Job 42:6).

Then Job replied to the Lord,
>*I am vile and ashamed to speak.*
>*I have no answer for You,*
>>*I cover my mouth and won't speak.*
>*Once I have said too much*
>>*So I won't make a second mistake*
>>*By talking too much.*
>>>Amen.

Chapters 40:6–41:33

GOD CHALLENGES JOB

AFTER Job humbles himself, God realizes Job has not come to the end of himself. God accuses Job of trying to "play God" by "trying to prove Me wrong, that you may be right." God challenges Job to demonstrate his power if he thinks he is equal to God, "Is your arm as strong as Mine?"

Now God asks 20 questions that demonstrate Job's finiteness. Job doesn't know the answers and he can't do what God does.

God uses two illustrations from His creation to demonstrate His power—the hippopotamus and the crocodile. These beasts are more powerful than any man, because they were created by a powerful God. This is a picture of how God shows His omnipotence.

The Lord answered Job out of the storm,
>Stand at attention like a man,
>I have some more questions that you must answer.
Are you trying to reverse My decisions,
>Are you trying to prove Me wrong
>That you may be right?
Is your arm as strong as Mine?
>Can your voice thunder like Mine?
If you think you can, then robe yourself in splendor
>And show your majesty.
Display your anger against sin
>And all who are proud
>To bring them down.
Let your glance punish the wicked,
>Walk on those who oppose you
>And bury them in the dust.
If you—Job—can do these things,
>You are strong enough to survive.

Look at the mighty hippopotamus,
>Just as I created you, I created it.
He eats grass like an ox,
>He has great strength in his loins
>And muscles in its stomach.
He moves his tail like a cedar,
>The muscles in his thighs are strong.
His bones are like bronze pipes,
>His limbs are like bars of iron;
>Only His creator can frighten Him.

The mountains grow food for the hippopotamus
    Where all the wild beasts live.
He lies quietly under the thorny lotus bushes,
    And is hidden by the reeds in the swamp.
He is not concerned when the floods rage,
    Even when the water rushes into his mouth.
Can anyone tame him to follow them?
    Can they lead him with a nose hook?
Amen.

Chapter 41

THE LORD CONTINUES

Can you fish for a crocodile with a hook,
    Can you tie his mouth with a rope?
Can you put a ring in its nose,
    And lead him about like a tamed animal?
Can you play with him like a house animal,
    Can you work him on the farm?
Could you put a string around its neck,
    And let little girls play with him?
Will merchants try to sell them,
    And would customers buy them?
Can an arrow penetrate his skin,
    And can a spear his head?
If you even touch one,
    You'll have such a terrible fight

You'd never want to do it again.
No, you can't capture the crocodile
    Without a great fight.
Since you wouldn't disturb a crocodile,
        Then who is able to stand up to Me?
        Who has ever fought against Me and prevailed?

I am describing the awesome power of the crocodile;
        He has strength throughout his huge body.
Who can penetrate his scales,
        Or open his massive jaws?
His protection is the row of scales,
        One so close to the other
        That no air can get through.
Light flashes out when he sneezes,
        He sees through the slits in his eyelids
        Like the sliver of the sun as it rises.
Steam rises from his nostrils
        Like a pot boiling on the fire.

The crocodile has a hard, strong neck
        That scares those who meet him in the way.
His heart is as hard as a stone,
        Even the mighty are afraid of him.
A sword is useless against him,
        Neither will arrows or spears harm him.
He bites through iron as if it were straw,
        And bronze as if it were rotten wood.
He doesn't run from arrows
        And stones from a slingshot are nothing;
        Clubs are useless, and he laughs at sticks.
His belly is slick like pottery,
        He easily glides across the mud.

The crocodile stirs the river like boiling water,
He leaves a wake when swimming.
There is no creature on earth like him,
He fears no one and no other animal.
He looks up at all the tall animals,
But he is king over these proud beasts.
Since I created the small and great
And put them all in their place,
Do not I have the right to do as I please
With people I have made on this earth?
Amen.

My Prayer

Lord, You have made everything for its purpose,
Everything is to glorify You.
Help me find my purpose and do it that I may glorify You.
Amen.

Chapter 42

JOB'S REPENTANCE AND RESTORATION

IF Job previously had any misunderstandings about the person of God, now he has full understanding. Previously, Job had secondhand knowledge of God, now Job knows God personally and firsthand. Job has experienced God. This is one of the purposes of this book, that you may know God in a real and experiential way.

After God had answered Job, he turned his attention to Job's three friends (we don't know why God ignored Elihu). God told the three they had not spoken correctly (Job 42:7). God called Job "My servant," acknowledging Job has a relationship with Him (Job 42:8). God commanded the three to take seven bulls (expensive) and get Job (the family priest) to sacrifice and pray for them because Job was their intercessor.

God healed Job and restored his fortune twofold. Satan was defeated and God was glorified. Job's sisters and brothers returned for a feast with Job, bringing gifts with them.

In due time Job had the same amount of children lost in the cyclone (Job 1:13,19). It is not stated in the text whether Job's wife, or a younger second wife, bore these children.

Since, *"Indeed the LORD gave Job twice as much as he had before"* (Job 42:10), then it is assumed Job was 70 when his trials hit; because afterward *"Job lived an hundred and forty years"* (Job 42:16). Since Job was the son of Issachar (Gen. 46:13) and a grandson of Jacob, his life stretched halfway through the 400 years the nation of Israel was in Egypt. It is possible that Moses met Job and received information to write the Book of Job.

Then Job replied to the Lord,
I now realize You can do everything
And no one can obstruct what You do.
You asked,
'Who is this that ignorantly wants to know what I can do?'
Then Job admitted to the Lord,
I asked foolish questions,
I did not understand Your wonders,
Your wisdom is far beyond me.
Lord, You told me to listen to Your questions;
You, Lord, told me I had to answer them.

I, Job, had only heard about You
  With the hearing of my ears.
But now I have seen with my eyes,
  Now I have experienced Your presence personally.
I'm sorry for my rash statement,
  I repent in dust and ashes.

Job has been identified in history as one of the most patient and godly men of the Old Testament (James 5:10-11). Thus, Job is our example when we go through trials and sufferings.

After the Lord finished speaking to Job,
  Then the Lord said to Eliphaz,
  The leader of the counselors,
My anger is directed toward you,
  And the two counselors with you,
Because what you said to Job was wrong;
  My servant Job said the right things about Me.

Now the three of you must get seven sacrifices,
  Give them to my servant, Job.
My servant, Job, will offer these sacrifices for you,
  And I will accept Job's intercession
  When he prays on your behalf.
I will not punish the three of you
  With the treatment you deserve,
For you have not spoken rightly about Me,
  As my servant, Job has demonstrated faith.

So Eliphaz, Bildad, and Zophar obeyed the Lord,
  And the Lord accepted Job's prayer for them.

After Job interceded for his counselors,
  The Lord restored his wealth,
  Giving him twice what he previously had.

Then Job's brothers, sisters, and former friends
    Returned to eat a meal in Job's home.
They comforted Job because of all the sufferings
    He had endured,
    Bringing him money and gifts.

Job's Unanswered Prayers

Job prayed for immediate death (Job 3:11; 10:18) but God didn't answer. Also, Job didn't get an answer to his prayer for God to curse the day he was born (Job 3:3-8). When believers are going through pain and suffering, they may say things they don't mean, and they may even pray wrongly for things that God doesn't want them to have. Then, after a person's trial is over, they may look back to see that God had better things in store for them than the things they asked. They may rejoice that God didn't answer their request. If God had taken Job's life, he wouldn't have become a great testimony of patience in trials, and he would not have enjoyed 140 years of prosperity (Job 42:16).

The Lord blessed Job's latter state
    More than before his trials,
    Giving him twice as much wealth.
Now Job had 14,000 sheep, 6,000 camels, 2,000 oxen
And 1,000 donkeys.
    He had seven more sons
    And three more daughters.

Job named the first daughter Jemimah,
    The second, Keziah,
    The third, Kereu-Hapukh.
Job's daughters were the most beautiful in the land,
    And he gave them an inheritance
    Along with their brothers.

After this, 70-year-old Job lived another 140 years;
> God doubly blessed his faith.

Job was able to see his sons and grandchildren
> Up to the fourth generation,
> Then Job died after having a long, good life.

(The Septuagint adds) And it is written
> That he shall rise again
> With those whom the Lord raises up.
>> Amen.

My Prayer

Lord, thank You for the promises of Your blessing
> *On those who trust and obey You.*
> *I claim these blessings for a good life down here*
> *On this earth*
>> *And for blessings in Heaven with You.*
>> *Amen.*

Conclusion

WHAT JOB KNEW
ABOUT GOD AND DOCTRINE

JOB was the first written book of the Bible, therefore, Job didn't know everything we know in this dispensation. He lived in the dawn of revelation; God has not yet given the Ten Commandments or directions for the different sacrifices or temple worship. Job didn't know the full revelation of God in the incarnation of Jesus Christ. Job knew God forgave sins, but he didn't know the implications of Christ's death.

Job had significant knowledge of God's omnipotence (power), omniscience (wisdom), and omnipresence (God's unlimited presence at every place in His creation). Job knew God sovereignly ruled both the temporal and spiritual world. God's providence was both direct and permissive.

The Book of Job teaches evil is personified in satan and that he hates God's people and delivers malice to them. Satan, however, is subject to God, reports to God, and can only do what God permits him to do. Yet, satan incessantly throws trials and temptations at God's children.

The Book of Job teaches that people are born in iniquity (Job 14:1-4) and are personal sinners. Job acknowledges the sins of his youth (Job 13:26).

Job believed in the resurrection of the body and knew he would see God after death (Job 13:15; 19:26) and that there will be future blessings to the righteous. The book of Job teaches a final judgment for unbelievers where they receive a just recompense for their evil deeds.

The Book of Job also teaches that man needs an intercessor to appeal to God on his behalf. God gives a man (Jesus, the God-Man) who will save people from their sin and act as mediator between God and man, *"For there is one God and one Mediator between God and men, the Man Christ Jesus"* (1 Tim. 2:5).

135

Job believed an offended God could only be approached by sacrifice—the type of sacrifices mentioned in the life of Abraham.

APPENDIX A

The Location of Uz

THE Book of Job begins, *"There was a man in the land of Uz whose name was Job"* (Job 1:1). We know the man, but no one knows for sure where Uz is located. Some think it was south of Israel, others think it was north of Israel. The arguments for both positions follow to give you information so you can decide.

Uz: South of Israel

Uz is mentioned first in Scripture as the eldest son of Aram, the grandson of Shem (Gen. 11:23). This is the biological line of Abraham and the Jews. Some think that a certain section of land was called Uz by the name of the man who colonized the area. Since Uz came from the Semites that implies the residents of the area are of the same blood and ethnic background as Abraham and God's children.

Uz is identified with several nations that are located south of Israel (Jer. 25:20) and Uz was subjected to the Edomites at one time (Lam. 4:21). The kingdom of Edom is south of the Dead Sea.

Job was *"the greatest of all the men of the east"* (Job 1:3), a geographical reference included by Moses indicating "the land of Uz" was east of Midian, and *"dwelt as a king in the army"* (Job 29:25). This land was later re-named Edom (Lam. 4:21), suggesting Uz was located in the eastern Sinai Desert.

Robert Allen of the *New American Commentary, Vol. II*, said, "The land of Uz, as best we can guess, was in the area of Northern Saudi Arabia or Southern Jordan.... Throughout the book are occasional references to farming, rivers and hills, none of which would disallow the light desert of the Edomite plateau. The thunder and lightning storms as well as the

137

unwelcomed east wind are characteristic of that area. Even hail, ice and snow mentioned several times are known to occur there."[1]

The Sabeans attacked Job's flocks and killed his servants. Sabeans are desert raiders who came from the Arabian Desert (Job 1:15,17), suggesting the land of Uz was located in proximity of the Sinai Peninsula.

Many scholars of past generations have said Moses wrote the Book of Job (E. W. Bullinger[2], B.H. Carroll[3], Henry Morris[4]), suggesting Job and Moses were in contact with each other (Job, the source of the book; Moses, the author). If Job is the son of Issachar (Gen. 46:13), he would have been about 20 years of age when Jacob and all his sons—including Issachar—went down to Egypt to begin Israel's 400 year sojourn in that country.

Job either returned from or stayed outside Egypt—in the Sinai Peninsula—when all other Israelites went to Egypt. From age 20 to age 50, Job accumulated his wealth; but he lost his wealth in his trials at age 70. After his trials were over, Job lived another 140 years (Job 42:10) which places him in the region of the Sinai Peninsula about the same time Moses is "run out" of Egypt. It's possible that Moses and Job crossed paths. During this encounter, Moses could have become an "ear-witness" to the stories of Job's temptation and Moses wrote down the stories. Also, Moses became an "eye-witness" to Job's prosperity and second family; hence, he was able to finish the story of Job's life where he "lived happily ever after."

Uz: North of Israel

Because of Job's advanced age, many scholars believe that Job lived in the Patriarchal Period when men lived longer than later when men lived approximately 70 years old (Ps. 90:10). Abraham lived to be 175 years old and Job lived to be 210 years old, living 70 years before his trials, plus an additional 140 years after his trials (Job 42:10).

Job had three friends who came to counsel him. They were a Tenanite, a Naamathite, and a Shuhite (Job 2:11). The Tenanites (Gen. 36:11) were often associated with Edom, so the presence of this man is an argument for Uz being in Southern Israel. However, the Naamathite is from Northern Israel as well as Shuhite, son of Shuah, who was the son of Keturah and Abraham (Gen. 25:2). There are several historical references placing "Suhu" in northern Israel.

J. G. Wetzstein journeyed to the area in North Israel between Mount Hermon and Damascus in A.D. 1862 and wrote a compelling essay to describe the area and analyzed claims that Job lived in the area.[5] Wetzstein included a map of the Monastery of Job that is located near the Golan territory. The map does not have a distinguishable scale of miles in English, but this would place Job's home some 40-50 miles from the Mediterranean Sea, accounting for Job's numerous references to the sea and ocean. Also, being on the northern territory of modern day Israel, would account for Job's knowledge of the Jordan River.

Wetzstein learned from the Arabs in the area there were three locations associated with Job. The first is the tomb of Job, Makam Ejub; the second is the village of Job, Der Ejuh; the third is the Monastery of Job.[6] I have been to the Holy Land on many occasions and know that many of the traditions locating biblical sites are suspect. We just can't verify their historical locations. However these locations associated with Job are both compelling and at the same time perplexing. After you read the following, you will agree that this could be the area where Job lived, or it might not be.

As Wetzstein toured the area, he heard many of the natives refer to Hauran as "Job's fatherland" and "The Land of Job." He was even pointed to "The Summer Palace of Job."[7] Later he was shown the area that was called "Job's pasture ground."

Wetzstein found a tradition that Job journeyed into Egypt to marry Rahmb, the daughter of Ephraim who had inherited the robe of beauty from her grandfather Joseph (was this worn by Joseph while serving Pharaoh?)[8]

Wetzstein said that the area was rich in wheat, corn, and other cereals. It also had well nourished pastures for cows and other cattle.[9]

When Wetzstein visited there, he described pilgrims coming from the Sudan to visit Mecca and Madenna; they also visited the Monastery of Job. "They washed themselves daily in Job's fountain and prayed upon Job's stone."[10]

When Wetzstein first visited the Monastery of Job, he found an inscription in stone, written in Greek, indicating it was carved "A.D. July 25, 536." The inscription noted "The Kingdom of Christ." Wetzstein believes the Monastery existed 536 years after Christ.

When Wetzstein visited the Monastery, it was inhabited by a sheikh named Ahmed El-Kadiri who had apparently rented it out from one of the khalis to whom the monastery belonged.

Eusebius, one of the early church fathers (a disciple of the apostle John), seemed to give some credibility to the claim that Job was from this area. He wrote in the book *Ononastikon*, "Astaroth Karnian is at present a very large village beyond the Jordan, in the province of Arabia, which is called Batanaea. Here, according to tradition, they affix the dwelling of Job."[11] Wetzstein also quotes Jerome (approximately A.D. 300) who also believed that this area includes "the home of Job."[12]

Wetzstein quoted Chrysostom, "Many pilgrims from the end of the earth come to Arabia, in order to seek for the dung hill on which Job lay, and with rapture to kiss the ground where he suffered."[13]

Chrysostom thinks the Monastery of Job came into existence between A. D. 200 and 250. Some say there were no monasteries built that early because monasteries did not appear until A.D. 350 However, we know the Essene community (of Dead Sea Scrolls fame), was building monasteries in the wilderness before the time of Christ. Therefore it is not speculation to think that the Monastery of Job was built somewhere between A.D. 200 and 250.

In a summary statement, Wetzstein located the land of Job at 32° 44-north latitude and 35° 51-45 latitude east (from Greenwich).[14]

Conclusion Possibilities

There are two different views about where Job's home is located—one in the south, the other in the north. I believe the one in the south has more biblical credibility, while the one in the north has more credibility from tradition.

Could it be there were two locations called Uz? Could it be that some early observers mistakenly thought the northern location is the home of Job because of the name? Could they have mistakenly "projected" the name Job on to towns, and pastures, and buildings?

Scholars do not agree on the location of Uz. *Nelson's Illustrated Bible Dictionary* makes this statement, "The exact location of the land of Uz is unknown."[15]

Both positions have been presented. You decide. Perhaps only God knows the exact location for sure.

Endnotes

1. Robert Allen, *The New American Commentary, Vol. II* (Nashville, TN: Broadman and Holman Publishers, 1993), 29.

2. E. W. Bullinger, *The Companion Bible* (Grand Rapids, MI: Kregal Publications, 1990), 666.

3. B. H. Carroll, *An Interpretation of the English Bible: The Poetical Books of the Bible* (Grand Rapids, MI: Baker Book House, 1948), 12.

4. Henry M. Morris, *The Defenders Study Bible* (Grand Rapids, MI: World Publishing, 2001), 565. Morris says "Uniform Jewish tradition ascribed the Book of Job to Moses.... Job himself was the original author (Job 18:23,24). Moses most likely came into possession of Job's record during his 40-year exile from Egypt in the land of Midian (not far from Job's own homeland in Uz), (Moses) editing it for the benefit of his own contempories.

5. J. G. Wetzstein, "The Monastery of Job in Huran and the Tradition of Job," A biblical commentary on the Book of Job by F. Delitzsch (Grand Rapids, MI: William B. Eerdmans Publishing Co., 1949), 395. Originally published from the original *Commentary on the Old Testmament* by Keil and Delitzsch, published in German in 1866.

6. Ibid., 395-415.

7. Ibid., 396.

8. Ibid., 397.

9. Ibid., 399.

10. Ibid., 405.

11. Ibid., 427.

12. Ibid., 429.

13. Ibid., 429.

14. Visit Google Earth at www.google.com for a closer look at the area.

15. Herbert Lockyer, Sr., *Nelson's Illustrated Bible Dictionary* (Nashville, TN: Thomas Nelson Publishers, 1986), 1083.

Appendix B

THE BOOK OF JOB

KING JAMES VERSION OF THE BIBLE

Chapter 1

[1] There was a man in the land of Uz, whose name was Job; and that man was perfect and upright, and one that feared God, and eschewed evil.

[2] And there were born unto him seven sons and three daughters.

[3] His substance also was seven thousand sheep, and three thousand camels, and five hundred yoke of oxen, and five hundred she asses, and a very great household; so that this man was the greatest of all the men of the east.

[4] And his sons went and feasted in their houses, every one his day; and sent and called for their three sisters to eat and to drink with them.

[5] And it was so, when the days of their feasting were gone about, that Job sent and sanctified them, and rose up early in the morning, and offered burnt offerings according to the number of them all: for Job said, It may be that my sons have sinned, and cursed God in their hearts. Thus did Job continually.

[6] Now there was a day when the sons of God came to present themselves before the LORD, and Satan came also among them.

[7] And the LORD said unto Satan, Whence comest thou? Then Satan answered the LORD, and said, From going to and fro in the earth, and from walking up and down in it.

[8] And the LORD said unto Satan, Hast thou considered my servant Job, that there is none like him in the earth, a perfect and an upright man, one that feareth God, and escheweth evil?

[9] Then Satan answered the LORD, and said, Doth Job fear God for nought?

[10] Hast not thou made an hedge about him, and about his house, and about all that he hath on every side? thou hast blessed the work of his hands, and his substance is increased in the land.

[11] But put forth thine hand now, and touch all that he hath, and he will curse thee to thy face.

[12] And the LORD said unto Satan, Behold, all that he hath is in thy power; only upon himself put not forth thine hand. So Satan went forth from the presence of the LORD.

[13] And there was a day when his sons and his daughters were eating and drinking wine in their eldest brother's house:

[14] And there came a messenger unto Job, and said, The oxen were plowing, and the asses feeding beside them:

[15] And the Sabeans fell upon them, and took them away; yea, they have slain the servants with the edge of the sword; and I only am escaped alone to tell thee.

[16] While he was yet speaking, there came also another, and said, The fire of God is fallen from heaven, and hath burned up the sheep, and the servants, and consumed them; and I only am escaped alone to tell thee.

[17] While he was yet speaking, there came also another, and said, The Chaldeans made out three bands, and fell upon the camels, and have carried them away, yea, and slain the servants with the edge of the sword; and I only am escaped alone to tell thee.

[18] While he was yet speaking, there came also another, and said, Thy sons and thy daughters were eating and drinking wine in their eldest brother's house:

[19] And, behold, there came a great wind from the wilderness, and smote the four corners of the house, and it fell upon the young men, and they are dead; and I only am escaped alone to tell thee.

[20] Then Job arose, and rent his mantle, and shaved his head, and fell down upon the ground, and worshipped,

[21] And said, Naked came I out of my mother's womb, and naked shall I return thither: the LORD gave, and the LORD hath taken away; blessed be the name of the LORD.

[22] In all this Job sinned not, nor charged God foolishly.

Chapter 2

[1] Again there was a day when the sons of God came to present themselves before the LORD, and Satan came also among them to present himself before the LORD.

[2] And the LORD said unto Satan, From whence comest thou? And Satan answered the LORD, and said, From going to and fro in the earth, and from walking up and down in it.

[3] And the LORD said unto Satan, Hast thou considered my servant Job, that there is none like him in the earth, a perfect and an upright man, one that feareth God, and escheweth evil? and still he holdeth fast his integrity, although thou movedst me against him, to destroy him without cause.

[4] And Satan answered the LORD, and said, Skin for skin, yea, all that a man hath will he give for his life.

[5] But put forth thine hand now, and touch his bone and his flesh, and he will curse thee to thy face.

[6] And the LORD said unto Satan, Behold, he is in thine hand; but save his life.

[7] So went Satan forth from the presence of the LORD, and smote Job

with sore boils from the sole of his foot unto his crown.

[8] And he took him a potsherd to scrape himself withal; and he sat down among the ashes.

[9] Then said his wife unto him, Dost thou still retain thine integrity? curse God, and die.

[10] But he said unto her, Thou speakest as one of the foolish women speaketh. What? shall we receive good at the hand of God, and shall we not receive evil? In all this did not Job sin with his lips.

[11] Now when Job's three friends heard of all this evil that was come upon him, they came every one from his own place; Eliphaz the Temanite, and Bildad the Shuhite, and Zophar the Naamathite: for they had made an appointment together to come to mourn with him and to comfort him.

[12] And when they lifted up their eyes afar off, and knew him not, they lifted up their voice, and wept; and they rent every one his mantle, and sprinkled dust upon their heads toward heaven.

[13] So they sat down with him upon the ground seven days and seven nights, and none spake a word unto him: for they saw that his grief was very great.

Chapter 3

[1] After this opened Job his mouth, and cursed his day.

[2] And Job spake, and said,

[3] Let the day perish wherein I was born, and the night in which it was said, There is a man child conceived.

[4] Let that day be darkness; let not God regard it from above, neither let the light shine upon it.

[5] Let darkness and the shadow of death stain it; let a cloud dwell upon it; let the blackness of the day terrify it.

[6] As for that night, let darkness seize upon it; let it not be joined unto the days of the year, let it not come into the number of the months.

[7] Lo, let that night be solitary, let no joyful voice come therein.

[8] Let them curse it that curse the day, who are ready to raise up their mourning.

[9] Let the stars of the twilight thereof be dark; let it look for light, but have none; neither let it see the dawning of the day:

[10] Because it shut not up the doors of my mother's womb, nor hid sorrow from mine eyes.

[11] Why died I not from the womb? why did I not give up the ghost when I came out of the belly?

[12] Why did the knees prevent me? or why the breasts that I should suck?

[13] For now should I have lain still and been quiet, I should have slept: then had I been at rest,

[14] With kings and counsellers of the earth, which built desolate places for themselves;

[15] Or with princes that had gold, who filled their houses with silver:

[16] Or as an hidden untimely birth I had not been; as infants which never saw light.

[17] There the wicked cease from troubling; and there the weary be at rest.

[18] There the prisoners rest together; they hear not the voice of the oppressor.

[19] The small and great are there; and the servant is free from his master.

[20] Wherefore is light given to him that is in misery, and life unto the bitter in soul;

[21] Which long for death, but it cometh not; and dig for it more than for hid treasures;

[22] Which rejoice exceedingly, and are glad, when they can find the grave?

[23] Why is light given to a man whose way is hid, and whom God hath hedged in?

[24] For my sighing cometh before I eat, and my roarings are poured out like the waters.

[25] For the thing which I greatly feared is come upon me, and that which I was afraid of is come unto me.

[26] I was not in safety, neither had I rest, neither was I quiet; yet trouble came.

Chapter 4

[1] Then Eliphaz the Temanite answered and said,

[2] If we assay to commune with thee, wilt thou be grieved? but who can withhold himself from speaking?

[3] Behold, thou hast instructed many, and thou hast strengthened the weak hands.

[4] Thy words have upholden him that was falling, and thou hast strengthened the feeble knees.

[5] But now it is come upon thee, and thou faintest; it toucheth thee, and thou art troubled.

[6] Is not this thy fear, thy confidence, thy hope, and the uprightness of thy ways?

[7] Remember, I pray thee, who ever perished, being innocent? or where were the righteous cut off?

[8] Even as I have seen, they that plow iniquity, and sow wickedness, reap the same.

[9] By the blast of God they perish, and by the breath of his nostrils are they consumed.

[10] The roaring of the lion, and the voice of the fierce lion, and the teeth of the young lions, are broken.

[11] The old lion perisheth for lack of prey, and the stout lion's whelps are scattered abroad.

[12] Now a thing was secretly brought to me, and mine ear received a little thereof.

[13] In thoughts from the visions of the night, when deep sleep falleth on men,

[14] Fear came upon me, and trembling, which made all my bones to shake.

[15] Then a spirit passed before my face; the hair of my flesh stood up:

[16] It stood still, but I could not discern the form thereof: an image was before mine eyes, there was silence, and I heard a voice, saying,

[17] Shall mortal man be more just than God? shall a man be more pure than his maker?

[18] Behold, he put no trust in his servants; and his angels he charged with folly:

[19] How much less in them that dwell in houses of clay, whose foundation is in the dust, which are crushed before the moth?

[20] They are destroyed from morning to evening: they perish for ever without any regarding it.

[21] Doth not their excellency which is in them go away? they die, even without wisdom.

Chapter 5

[1] Call now, if there be any that will answer thee; and to which of the saints wilt thou turn?

[2] For wrath killeth the foolish man, and envy slayeth the silly one.

[3] I have seen the foolish taking root: but suddenly I cursed his habitation.

[4] His children are far from safety, and they are crushed in the gate, neither is there any to deliver them.

[5] Whose harvest the hungry eateth up, and taketh it even out of the thorns, and the robber swalloweth up their substance.

[6] Although affliction cometh not forth of the dust, neither doth trouble spring out of the ground;

[7] Yet man is born unto trouble, as the sparks fly upward.

[8] I would seek unto God, and unto God would I commit my cause:

[9] Which doeth great things and unsearchable; marvellous things without number:

[10] Who giveth rain upon the earth, and sendeth waters upon the fields:

[11] To set up on high those that be low; that those which mourn may be exalted to safety.

[12] He disappointeth the devices of the crafty, so that their hands cannot perform their enterprise.

[13] He taketh the wise in their own craftiness: and the counsel of the froward is carried headlong.

[14] They meet with darkness in the daytime, and grope in the noonday as in the night.

[15] But he saveth the poor from the sword, from their mouth, and from the hand of the mighty.

[16] So the poor hath hope, and iniquity stoppeth her mouth.

[17] Behold, happy is the man whom God correcteth: therefore despise not thou the chastening of the Almighty:

[18] For he maketh sore, and bindeth up: he woundeth, and his hands make whole.

[19] He shall deliver thee in six troubles: yea, in seven there shall no evil touch thee.

[20] In famine he shall redeem thee from death: and in war from the power of the sword.

[21] Thou shalt be hid from the scourge of the tongue: neither shalt thou be afraid of destruction when it cometh.

[22] At destruction and famine thou shalt laugh: neither shalt thou be afraid of the beasts of the earth.

[23] For thou shalt be in league with the stones of the field: and the beasts of the field shall be at peace with thee.

[24] And thou shalt know that thy tabernacle shall be in peace; and thou shalt visit thy habitation, and shalt not sin.

[25] Thou shalt know also that thy seed shall be great, and thine offspring as the grass of the earth.

[26] Thou shalt come to thy grave in a full age, like as a shock of corn cometh in in his season.

[27] Lo this, we have searched it, so it is; hear it, and know thou it for thy good.

Chapter 6

[1] But Job answered and said,

[2] Oh that my grief were throughly weighed, and my calamity laid in the balances together!

[3] For now it would be heavier than the sand of the sea: therefore my words are swallowed up.

[4] For the arrows of the Almighty are within me, the poison whereof drinketh up my spirit: the terrors of God do set themselves in array against me.

[5] Doth the wild ass bray when he hath grass? or loweth the ox over his fodder?

[6] Can that which is unsavoury be eaten without salt? or is there any taste in the white of an egg?

[7] The things that my soul refused to touch are as my sorrowful meat.

[8] Oh that I might have my request; and that God would grant me the thing that I long for!

[9] Even that it would please God to destroy me; that he would let loose his hand, and cut me off!

[10] Then should I yet have comfort; yea, I would harden myself in sorrow: let him not spare; for I have not concealed the words of the Holy One.

[11] What is my strength, that I should hope? and what is mine end, that I should prolong my life?

[12] Is my strength the strength of stones? or is my flesh of brass?

[13] Is not my help in me? and is wisdom driven quite from me?

[14] To him that is afflicted pity should be shewed from his friend; but he forsaketh the fear of the Almighty.

[15] My brethren have dealt deceitfully as a brook, and as the stream of brooks they pass away;

[16] Which are blackish by reason of the ice, and wherein the snow is hid:

[17] What time they wax warm, they vanish: when it is hot, they are consumed out of their place.

[18] The paths of their way are turned aside; they go to nothing, and perish.

[19] The troops of Tema looked, the companies of Sheba waited for them.

[20] They were confounded because they had hoped; they came thither, and were ashamed.

[21] For now ye are nothing; ye see my casting down, and are afraid.

[22] Did I say, Bring unto me? or, Give a reward for me of your substance?

[23] Or, Deliver me from the enemy's hand? or, Redeem me from the hand of the mighty?

[24] Teach me, and I will hold my tongue: and cause me to understand wherein I have erred.

[25] How forcible are right words! but what doth your arguing reprove?

[26] Do ye imagine to reprove words, and the speeches of one that is desperate, which are as wind?

[27] Yea, ye overwhelm the fatherless, and ye dig a pit for your friend.

[28] Now therefore be content, look upon me; for it is evident unto you if I lie.

[29] Return, I pray you, let it not be iniquity; yea, return again, my righteousness is in it.

[30] Is there iniquity in my tongue? cannot my taste discern perverse things?

Chapter 7

[1] Is there not an appointed time to man upon earth? are not his days also like the days of an hireling?

[2] As a servant earnestly desireth the shadow, and as an hireling looketh for the reward of his work:

[3] So am I made to possess months of vanity, and wearisome nights are appointed to me.

[4] When I lie down, I say, When shall I arise, and the night be gone? and I am full of tossings to and fro unto the dawning of the day.

[5] My flesh is clothed with worms and clods of dust; my skin is broken, and become loathsome.

[6] My days are swifter than a weaver's shuttle, and are spent without hope.

[7] O remember that my life is wind: mine eye shall no more see good.

[8] The eye of him that hath seen me shall see me no more: thine eyes are upon me, and I am not.

[9] As the cloud is consumed and vanisheth away: so he that goeth down to the grave shall come up no more.

[10] He shall return no more to his house, neither shall his place know him any more.

[11] Therefore I will not refrain my mouth; I will speak in the anguish of my spirit; I will complain in the bitterness of my soul.

[12] Am I a sea, or a whale, that thou settest a watch over me?

[13] When I say, My bed shall comfort me, my couch shall ease my complaint;

[14] Then thou scarest me with dreams, and terrifiest me through visions:

[15] So that my soul chooseth strangling, and death rather than my life.

[16] I loathe it; I would not live always: let me alone; for my days are vanity.

[17] What is man, that thou shouldest magnify him? and that thou shouldest set thine heart upon him?

[18] And that thou shouldest visit him every morning, and try him every moment?

[19] How long wilt thou not depart from me, nor let me alone till I swallow down my spittle?

[20] I have sinned; what shall I do unto thee, O thou preserver of men? why hast thou set me as a mark against thee, so that I am a burden to myself?

[21] And why dost thou not pardon my transgression, and take away mine iniquity? for now shall I sleep in the dust; and thou shalt seek me in the morning, but I shall not be.

Chapter 8

[1] Then answered Bildad the Shuhite, and said,

[2] How long wilt thou speak these things? and how long shall the words of thy mouth be like a strong wind?

[3] Doth God pervert judgment? or doth the Almighty pervert justice?

[4] If thy children have sinned against him, and he have cast them away for their transgression;

[5] If thou wouldest seek unto God betimes, and make thy supplication to the Almighty;

[6] If thou wert pure and upright; surely now he would awake for thee, and make the habitation of thy righteousness prosperous.

[7] Though thy beginning was small, yet thy latter end should greatly increase.

[8] For inquire, I pray thee, of the former age, and prepare thyself to the search of their fathers:

[9] (For we are but of yesterday, and know nothing, because our days upon earth are a shadow:)

[10] Shall not they teach thee, and tell thee, and utter words out of their heart?

[11] Can the rush grow up without mire? can the flag grow without water?

[12] Whilst it is yet in his greenness, and not cut down, it withereth before any other herb.

[13] So are the paths of all that forget God; and the hypocrite's hope shall perish:

[14] Whose hope shall be cut off, and whose trust shall be a spider's web.

[15] He shall lean upon his house, but it shall not stand: he shall hold it fast, but it shall not endure.

[16] He is green before the sun, and his branch shooteth forth in his garden.

[17] His roots are wrapped about the heap, and seeth the place of stones.

[18] If he destroy him from his place, then it shall deny him, saying, I have not seen thee.

[19] Behold, this is the joy of his way, and out of the earth shall others grow.

[20] Behold, God will not cast away a perfect man, neither will he help the evil doers:

[21] Till he fill thy mouth with laughing, and thy lips with rejoicing.

[22] They that hate thee shall be clothed with shame; and the dwellingplace of the wicked shall come to nought.

Chapter 9

[1] Then Job answered and said,

[2] I know it is so of a truth: but how should man be just with God?

[3] If he will contend with him, he cannot answer him one of a thousand.

[4] He is wise in heart, and mighty in strength: who hath hardened himself against him, and hath prospered?

[5] Which removeth the mountains, and they know not: which overturneth them in his anger.

[6] Which shaketh the earth out of her place, and the pillars thereof tremble.

[7] Which commandeth the sun, and it riseth not; and sealeth up the stars.

[8] Which alone spreadeth out the heavens, and treadeth upon the waves of the sea.

[9] Which maketh Arcturus, Orion, and Pleiades, and the chambers of the south.

[10] Which doeth great things past finding out; yea, and wonders without number.

[11] Lo, he goeth by me, and I see him not: he passeth on also, but I perceive him not.

[12] Behold, he taketh away, who can hinder him? who will say unto him, What doest thou?

[13] If God will not withdraw his anger, the proud helpers do stoop under him.

[14] How much less shall I answer him, and choose out my words to reason with him?

[15] Whom, though I were righteous, yet would I not answer, but I would make supplication to my judge.

[16] If I had called, and he had answered me; yet would I not believe that he had hearkened unto my voice.

[17] For he breaketh me with a tempest, and multiplieth my wounds without cause.

[18] He will not suffer me to take my breath, but filleth me with bitterness.

[19] If I speak of strength, lo, he is strong: and if of judgment, who shall set me a time to plead?

[20] If I justify myself, mine own mouth shall condemn me: if I say, I am perfect, it shall also prove me perverse.

[21] Though I were perfect, yet would I not know my soul: I would despise my life.

[22] This is one thing, therefore I said it, He destroyeth the perfect and the wicked.

[23] If the scourge slay suddenly, he will laugh at the trial of the innocent.

[24] The earth is given into the hand of the wicked: he covereth the faces of the judges thereof; if not, where, and who is he?

[25] Now my days are swifter than a post: they flee away, they see no good.

[26] They are passed away as the swift ships: as the eagle that hasteth to the prey.

[27] If I say, I will forget my complaint, I will leave off my heaviness, and comfort myself:

[28] I am afraid of all my sorrows, I know that thou wilt not hold me innocent.

[29] If I be wicked, why then labour I in vain?

[30] If I wash myself with snow water, and make my hands never so clean;

[31] Yet shalt thou plunge me in the ditch, and mine own clothes shall abhor me.

[32] For he is not a man, as I am, that I should answer him, and we should come together in judgment.

[33] Neither is there any daysman betwixt us, that might lay his hand upon us both.

[34] Let him take his rod away from me, and let not his fear terrify me:

[35] Then would I speak, and not fear him; but it is not so with me.

Chapter 10

[1] My soul is weary of my life; I will leave my complaint upon myself; I will speak in the bitterness of my soul.

[2] I will say unto God, Do not condemn me; shew me wherefore thou contendest with me.

[3] Is it good unto thee that thou shouldest oppress, that thou shouldest despise the work of thine hands, and shine upon the counsel of the wicked?

[4] Hast thou eyes of flesh? or seest thou as man seeth?

[5] Are thy days as the days of man? are thy years as man's days,

[6] That thou inquirest after mine iniquity, and searchest after my sin?

[7] Thou knowest that I am not wicked; and there is none that can deliver out of thine hand.

[8] Thine hands have made me and fashioned me together round about; yet thou dost destroy me.

[9] Remember, I beseech thee, that thou hast made me as the clay; and wilt thou bring me into dust again?

[10] Hast thou not poured me out as milk, and curdled me like cheese?

[11] Thou hast clothed me with skin and flesh, and hast fenced me with bones and sinews.

[12] Thou hast granted me life and favour, and thy visitation hath preserved my spirit.

[13] And these things hast thou hid in thine heart: I know that this is with thee.

[14] If I sin, then thou markest me, and thou wilt not acquit me from mine iniquity.

[15] If I be wicked, woe unto me; and if I be righteous, yet will I not lift up my head. I am full of confusion; therefore see thou mine affliction;

[16] For it increaseth. Thou huntest me as a fierce lion: and again thou shewest thyself marvellous upon me.

[17] Thou renewest thy witnesses against me, and increasest thine indignation upon me; changes and war are against me.

[18] Wherefore then hast thou brought me forth out of the womb? Oh that I had given up the ghost, and no eye had seen me!

[19] I should have been as though I had not been; I should have been carried from the womb to the grave.

[20] Are not my days few? cease then, and let me alone, that I may take comfort a little,

[21] Before I go whence I shall not return, even to the land of darkness and the shadow of death;

[22] A land of darkness, as darkness itself; and of the shadow of death, without any order, and where the light is as darkness.

Chapter 11

[1] Then answered Zophar the Naamathite, and said,

[2] Should not the multitude of words be answered? and should a man full of talk be justified?

[3] Should thy lies make men hold their peace? and when thou mockest, shall no man make thee ashamed?

[4] For thou hast said, My doctrine is pure, and I am clean in thine eyes.

[5] But oh that God would speak, and open his lips against thee;

[6] And that he would shew thee the secrets of wisdom, that they are double to that which is! Know therefore that God exacteth of thee less than thine iniquity deserveth.

[7] Canst thou by searching find out God? canst thou find out the Almighty unto perfection?

[8] It is as high as heaven; what canst thou do? deeper than hell; what canst thou know?

[9] The measure thereof is longer than the earth, and broader than the sea.

[10] If he cut off, and shut up, or gather together, then who can hinder him?

[11] For he knoweth vain men: he seeth wickedness also; will he not then consider it?

[12] For vain man would be wise, though man be born like a wild ass's colt.

[13] If thou prepare thine heart, and stretch out thine hands toward him;

[14] If iniquity be in thine hand, put it far away, and let not wickedness dwell in thy tabernacles.

[15] For then shalt thou lift up thy face without spot; yea, thou shalt be sted-fast, and shalt not fear:

[16] Because thou shalt forget thy mis-ery, and remember it as waters that pass away:

[17] And thine age shall be clearer than the noonday; thou shalt shine forth, thou shalt be as the morning.

[18] And thou shalt be secure, because there is hope; yea, thou shalt dig about thee, and thou shalt take thy rest in safety.

[19] Also thou shalt lie down, and none shall make thee afraid; yea, many shall make suit unto thee.

[20] But the eyes of the wicked shall fail, and they shall not escape, and their hope shall be as the giving up of the ghost.

Chapter 12

[1] And Job answered and said,

[2] No doubt but ye are the people, and wisdom shall die with you.

[3] But I have understanding as well as you; I am not inferior to you: yea, who knoweth not such things as these?

[4] I am as one mocked of his neigh-bour, who calleth upon God, and he answereth him: the just upright man is laughed to scorn.

[5] He that is ready to slip with his feet is as a lamp despised in the thought of him that is at ease.

[6] The tabernacles of robbers prosper, and they that provoke God are secure; into whose hand God bringeth abundantly.

[7] But ask now the beasts, and they shall teach thee; and the fowls of the air, and they shall tell thee:

[8] Or speak to the earth, and it shall teach thee: and the fishes of the sea shall declare unto thee.

[9] Who knoweth not in all these that the hand of the LORD hath wrought this?

[10] In whose hand is the soul of every living thing, and the breath of all mankind.

[11] Doth not the ear try words? and the mouth taste his meat?

[12] With the ancient is wisdom; and in length of days understanding.

[13] With him is wisdom and strength, he hath counsel and understanding.

[14] Behold, he breaketh down, and it cannot be built again: he shutteth up a man, and there can be no opening.

[15] Behold, he withholdeth the waters, and they dry up: also he sendeth them out, and they overturn the earth.

[16] With him is strength and wisdom: the deceived and the deceiver are his.

[17] He leadeth counsellers away spoiled, and maketh the judges fools.

[18] He looseth the bond of kings, and girdeth their loins with a girdle.

[19] He leadeth princes away spoiled, and overthroweth the mighty.

[20] He removeth away the speech of the trusty, and taketh away the understanding of the aged.

[21] He poureth contempt upon princes, and weakeneth the strength of the mighty.

[22] He discovereth deep things out of darkness, and bringeth out to light the shadow of death.

[23] He increaseth the nations, and destroyeth them: he enlargeth the nations, and straiteneth them again.

[24] He taketh away the heart of the chief of the people of the earth, and causeth them to wander in a wilderness where there is no way.

[25] They grope in the dark without light, and he maketh them to stagger like a drunken man.

Chapter 13

[1] Lo, mine eye hath seen all this, mine ear hath heard and understood it.

[2] What ye know, the same do I know also: I am not inferior unto you.

[3] Surely I would speak to the Almighty, and I desire to reason with God.

[4] But ye are forgers of lies, ye are all physicians of no value.

[5] O that ye would altogether hold your peace! and it should be your wisdom.

[6] Hear now my reasoning, and hearken to the pleadings of my lips.

[7] Will ye speak wickedly for God? and talk deceitfully for him?

[8] Will ye accept his person? will ye contend for God?

[9] Is it good that he should search you out? or as one man mocketh another, do ye so mock him?

[10] He will surely reprove you, if ye do secretly accept persons.

[11] Shall not his excellency make you afraid? and his dread fall upon you?

[12] Your remembrances are like unto ashes, your bodies to bodies of clay.

[13] Hold your peace, let me alone, that I may speak, and let come on me what will.

[14] Wherefore do I take my flesh in my teeth, and put my life in mine hand?

[15] Though he slay me, yet will I trust in him: but I will maintain mine own ways before him.

[16] He also shall be my salvation: for an hypocrite shall not come before him.

[17] Hear diligently my speech, and my declaration with your ears.

[18] Behold now, I have ordered my cause; I know that I shall be justified.

[19] Who is he that will plead with me? for now, if I hold my tongue, I shall give up the ghost.

[20] Only do not two things unto me: then will I not hide myself from thee.

[21] Withdraw thine hand far from me: and let not thy dread make me afraid.

[22] Then call thou, and I will answer: or let me speak, and answer thou me.

[23] How many are mine iniquities and sins? make me to know my transgression and my sin.

[24] Wherefore hidest thou thy face, and holdest me for thine enemy?

[25] Wilt thou break a leaf driven to and fro? and wilt thou pursue the dry stubble?

[26] For thou writest bitter things against me, and makest me to possess the iniquities of my youth.

[27] Thou puttest my feet also in the stocks, and lookest narrowly unto all my paths; thou settest a print upon the heels of my feet.

[28] And he, as a rotten thing, consumeth, as a garment that is motheaten.

Chapter 14

[1] Man that is born of a woman is of few days, and full of trouble.

[2] He cometh forth like a flower, and is cut down: he fleeth also as a shadow, and continueth not.

[3] And dost thou open thine eyes upon such an one, and bringest me into judgment with thee?

[4] Who can bring a clean thing out of an unclean? not one.

[5] Seeing his days are determined, the number of his months are with thee, thou hast appointed his bounds that he cannot pass;

[6] Turn from him, that he may rest, till he shall accomplish, as an hireling, his day.

[7] For there is hope of a tree, if it be cut down, that it will sprout again, and that the tender branch thereof will not cease.

[8] Though the root thereof wax old in the earth, and the stock thereof die in the ground;

[9] Yet through the scent of water it will bud, and bring forth boughs like a plant.

[10] But man dieth, and wasteth away: yea, man giveth up the ghost, and where is he?

[11] As the waters fail from the sea, and the flood decayeth and drieth up:

[12] So man lieth down, and riseth not: till the heavens be no more, they shall not awake, nor be raised out of their sleep.

[13] O that thou wouldest hide me in the grave, that thou wouldest keep me secret, until thy wrath be past, that thou wouldest appoint me a set time, and remember me!

[14] If a man die, shall he live again? all the days of my appointed time will I wait, till my change come.

[15] Thou shalt call, and I will answer thee: thou wilt have a desire to the work of thine hands.

[16] For now thou numberest my steps: dost thou not watch over my sin?

[17] My transgression is sealed up in a bag, and thou sewest up mine iniquity.

[18] And surely the mountain falling cometh to nought, and the rock is removed out of his place.

[19] The waters wear the stones: thou washest away the things which grow out of the dust of the earth; and thou destroyest the hope of man.

[20] Thou prevailest for ever against him, and he passeth: thou changest his countenance, and sendest him away.

[21] His sons come to honour, and he knoweth it not; and they are brought low, but he perceiveth it not of them.

[22] But his flesh upon him shall have pain, and his soul within him shall mourn.

Chapter 15

[1] Then answered Eliphaz the Temanite, and said,

[2] Should a wise man utter vain knowledge, and fill his belly with the east wind?

[3] Should he reason with unprofitable talk? or with speeches wherewith he can do no good?

[4] Yea, thou castest off fear, and restrainest prayer before God.

[5] For thy mouth uttereth thine iniquity, and thou choosest the tongue of the crafty.

[6] Thine own mouth condemneth thee, and not I: yea, thine own lips testify against thee.

[7] Art thou the first man that was born? or wast thou made before the hills?

[8] Hast thou heard the secret of God? and dost thou restrain wisdom to thyself?

[9] What knowest thou, that we know not? what understandest thou, which is not in us?

[10] With us are both the grayheaded and very aged men, much elder than thy father.

[11] Are the consolations of God small with thee? is there any secret thing with thee?

[12] Why doth thine heart carry thee away? and what do thy eyes wink at,

[13] That thou turnest thy spirit against God, and lettest such words go out of thy mouth?

[14] What is man, that he should be clean? and he which is born of a woman, that he should be righteous?

[15] Behold, he putteth no trust in his saints; yea, the heavens are not clean in his sight.

[16] How much more abominable and filthy is man, which drinketh iniquity like water?

[17] I will shew thee, hear me; and that which I have seen I will declare;

[18] Which wise men have told from their fathers, and have not hid it:

[19] Unto whom alone the earth was given, and no stranger passed among them.

[20] The wicked man travaileth with pain all his days, and the number of years is hidden to the oppressor.

[21] A dreadful sound is in his ears: in prosperity the destroyer shall come upon him.

[22] He believeth not that he shall return out of darkness, and he is waited for of the sword.

[23] He wandereth abroad for bread, saying, Where is it? he knoweth that the day of darkness is ready at his hand.

[24] Trouble and anguish shall make him afraid; they shall prevail against him, as a king ready to the battle.

[25] For he stretcheth out his hand against God, and strengtheneth himself against the Almighty.

[26] He runneth upon him, even on his neck, upon the thick bosses of his bucklers:

[27] Because he covereth his face with his fatness, and maketh collops of fat on his flanks.

[28] And he dwelleth in desolate cities, and in houses which no man inhabiteth, which are ready to become heaps.

[29] He shall not be rich, neither shall his substance continue, neither shall he prolong the perfection thereof upon the earth.

[30] He shall not depart out of darkness; the flame shall dry up his branches, and by the breath of his mouth shall he go away.

[31] Let not him that is deceived trust in vanity: for vanity shall be his recompence.

[32] It shall be accomplished before his time, and his branch shall not be green.

[33] He shall shake off his unripe grape as the vine, and shall cast off his flower as the olive.

[34] For the congregation of hypocrites shall be desolate, and fire shall consume the tabernacles of bribery.

[35] They conceive mischief, and bring forth vanity, and their belly prepareth deceit.

Chapter 16

[1] Then Job answered and said,

[2] I have heard many such things: miserable comforters are ye all.

[3] Shall vain words have an end? or what emboldeneth thee that thou answerest?

[4] I also could speak as ye do: if your soul were in my soul's stead, I could heap up words against you, and shake mine head at you.

[5] But I would strengthen you with my mouth, and the moving of my lips should asswage your grief.

[6] Though I speak, my grief is not asswaged: and though I forbear, what am I eased?

[7] But now he hath made me weary: thou hast made desolate all my company.

[8] And thou hast filled me with wrinkles, which is a witness against me: and my leanness rising up in me beareth witness to my face.

[9] He teareth me in his wrath, who hateth me: he gnasheth upon me with his teeth; mine enemy sharpeneth his eyes upon me.

[10] They have gaped upon me with their mouth; they have smitten me upon the cheek reproachfully; they have gathered themselves together against me.

[11] God hath delivered me to the ungodly, and turned me over into the hands of the wicked.

[12] I was at ease, but he hath broken me asunder: he hath also taken me by my neck, and shaken me to pieces, and set me up for his mark.

[13] His archers compass me round about, he cleaveth my reins asunder, and doth not spare; he poureth out my gall upon the ground.

[14] He breaketh me with breach upon breach, he runneth upon me like a giant.

[15] I have sewed sackcloth upon my skin, and defiled my horn in the dust.

[16] My face is foul with weeping, and on my eyelids is the shadow of death;

[17] Not for any injustice in mine hands: also my prayer is pure.

[18] O earth, cover not thou my blood, and let my cry have no place.

[19] Also now, behold, my witness is in heaven, and my record is on high.

[20] My friends scorn me: but mine eye poureth out tears unto God.

[21] O that one might plead for a man with God, as a man pleadeth for his neighbour!

[22] When a few years are come, then I shall go the way whence I shall not return.

Chapter 17

[1] My breath is corrupt, my days are extinct, the graves are ready for me.

[2] Are there not mockers with me? and doth not mine eye continue in their provocation?

[3] Lay down now, put me in a surety with thee; who is he that will strike hands with me?

[4] For thou hast hid their heart from understanding: therefore shalt thou not exalt them.

[5] He that speaketh flattery to his friends, even the eyes of his children shall fail.

[6] He hath made me also a byword of the people; and aforetime I was as a tabret.

[7] Mine eye also is dim by reason of sorrow, and all my members are as a shadow.

[8] Upright men shall be astonied at this, and the innocent shall stir up himself against the hypocrite.

[9] The righteous also shall hold on his way, and he that hath clean hands shall be stronger and stronger.

[10] But as for you all, do ye return, and come now: for I cannot find one wise man among you.

[11] My days are past, my purposes are broken off, even the thoughts of my heart.

[12] They change the night into day: the light is short because of darkness.

[13] If I wait, the grave is mine house: I have made my bed in the darkness.

[14] I have said to corruption, Thou art my father: to the worm, Thou are my mother, and my sister.

[15] And where is now my hope? as for my hope, who shall see it?

[16] They shall go down to the bars of the pit, when our rest together is in the dust.

Chapter 18

[1] Then answered Bildad the Shuhite, and said,

[2] How long will it be ere ye make an end of words? mark, and afterwards we will speak.

[3] Wherefore are we counted as beasts, and reputed vile in your sight?

[4] He teareth himself in his anger: shall the earth be forsaken for thee? and shall the rock be removed out of his place?

[5] Yea, the light of the wicked shall be put out, and the spark of his fire shall not shine.

[6] The light shall be dark in his tabernacle, and his candle shall be put out with him.

[7] The steps of his strength shall be straitened, and his own counsel shall cast him down.

[8] For he is cast into a net by his own feet, and he walketh upon a snare.

[9] The gin shall take him by the heel, and the robber shall prevail against him.

[10] The snare is laid for him in the ground, and a trap for him in the way.

[11] Terrors shall make him afraid on every side, and shall drive him to his feet.

[12] His strength shall be hungerbitten, and destruction shall be ready at his side.

[13] It shall devour the strength of his skin: even the firstborn of death shall devour his strength.

[14] His confidence shall be rooted out of his tabernacle, and it shall bring him to the king of terrors.

[15] It shall dwell in his tabernacle, because it is none of his: brimstone shall be scattered upon his habitation.

[16] His roots shall be dried up beneath, and above shall his branch be cut off.

[17] His remembrance shall perish from the earth, and he shall have no name in the street.

[18] He shall be driven from light into darkness, and chased out of the world.

[19] He shall neither have son nor nephew among his people, nor any remaining in his dwellings.

[20] They that come after him shall be astonied at his day, as they that went before were affrighted.

[21] Surely such are the dwellings of the wicked, and this is the place of him that knoweth not God.

Chapter 19

[1] Then Job answered and said,

[2] How long will ye vex my soul, and break me in pieces with words?

[3] These ten times have ye reproached me: ye are not ashamed that ye make yourselves strange to me.

[4] And be it indeed that I have erred, mine error remaineth with myself.

[5] If indeed ye will magnify yourselves against me, and plead against me my reproach:

[6] Know now that God hath overthrown me, and hath compassed me with his net.

[7] Behold, I cry out of wrong, but I am not heard: I cry aloud, but there is no judgment.

[8] He hath fenced up my way that I cannot pass, and he hath set darkness in my paths.

[9] He hath stripped me of my glory, and taken the crown from my head.

[10] He hath destroyed me on every side, and I am gone: and mine hope hath he removed like a tree.

[11] He hath also kindled his wrath against me, and he counteth me unto him as one of his enemies.

[12] His troops come together, and raise up their way against me, and encamp round about my tabernacle.

[13] He hath put my brethren far from me, and mine acquaintance are verily estranged from me.

[14] My kinsfolk have failed, and my familiar friends have forgotten me.

[15] They that dwell in mine house, and my maids, count me for a stranger: I am an alien in their sight.

[16] I called my servant, and he gave me no answer; I entreated him with my mouth.

[17] My breath is strange to my wife, though I entreated for the children's sake of mine own body.

[18] Yea, young children despised me; I arose, and they spake against me.

[19] All my inward friends abhorred me: and they whom I loved are turned against me.

[20] My bone cleaveth to my skin and to my flesh, and I am escaped with the skin of my teeth.

[21] Have pity upon me, have pity upon me, O ye my friends; for the hand of God hath touched me.

[22] Why do ye persecute me as God, and are not satisfied with my flesh?

[23] Oh that my words were now written! oh that they were printed in a book!

[24] That they were graven with an iron pen and lead in the rock for ever!

[25] For I know that my redeemer liveth, and that he shall stand at the latter day upon the earth:

[26] And though after my skin worms destroy this body, yet in my flesh shall I see God:

[27] Whom I shall see for myself, and mine eyes shall behold, and not another; though my reins be consumed within me.

[28] But ye should say, Why persecute we him, seeing the root of the matter is found in me?

[29] Be ye afraid of the sword: for wrath bringeth the punishments of the sword, that ye may know there is a judgment.

Chapter 20

[1] Then answered Zophar the Naamathite, and said,

[2] Therefore do my thoughts cause me to answer, and for this I make haste.

[3] I have heard the check of my reproach, and the spirit of my understanding causeth me to answer.

[4] Knowest thou not this of old, since man was placed upon earth,

[5] That the triumphing of the wicked is short, and the joy of the hypocrite but for a moment?

[6] Though his excellency mount up to the heavens, and his head reach unto the clouds;

[7] Yet he shall perish for ever like his own dung: they which have seen him shall say, Where is he?

[8] He shall fly away as a dream, and shall not be found: yea, he shall be chased away as a vision of the night.

[9] The eye also which saw him shall see him no more; neither shall his place any more behold him.

[10] His children shall seek to please the poor, and his hands shall restore their goods.

[11] His bones are full of the sin of his youth, which shall lie down with him in the dust.

[12] Though wickedness be sweet in his mouth, though he hide it under his tongue;

[13] Though he spare it, and forsake it not; but keep it still within his mouth:

[14] Yet his meat in his bowels is turned, it is the gall of asps within him.

[15] He hath swallowed down riches, and he shall vomit them up again: God shall cast them out of his belly.

[16] He shall suck the poison of asps: the viper's tongue shall slay him.

[17] He shall not see the rivers, the floods, the brooks of honey and butter.

[18] That which he laboured for shall he restore, and shall not swallow it down: according to his substance shall the restitution be, and he shall not rejoice therein.

[19] Because he hath oppressed and hath forsaken the poor; because he hath violently taken away an house which he builded not;

[20] Surely he shall not feel quietness in his belly, he shall not save of that which he desired.

[21] There shall none of his meat be left; therefore shall no man look for his goods.

[22] In the fulness of his sufficiency he shall be in straits: every hand of the wicked shall come upon him.

[23] When he is about to fill his belly, God shall cast the fury of his wrath upon him, and shall rain it upon him while he is eating.

[24] He shall flee from the iron weapon, and the bow of steel shall strike him through.

[25] It is drawn, and cometh out of the body; yea, the glittering sword cometh out of his gall: terrors are upon him.

[26] All darkness shall be hid in his secret places: a fire not blown shall consume him; it shall go ill with him that is left in his tabernacle.

[27] The heaven shall reveal his iniquity; and the earth shall rise up against him.

[28] The increase of his house shall depart, and his goods shall flow away in the day of his wrath.

[29] This is the portion of a wicked man from God, and the heritage appointed unto him by God.

Chapter 21

[1] But Job answered and said,

[2] Hear diligently my speech, and let this be your consolations.

[3] Suffer me that I may speak; and after that I have spoken, mock on.

[4] As for me, is my complaint to man? and if it were so, why should not my spirit be troubled?

[5] Mark me, and be astonished, and lay your hand upon your mouth.

[6] Even when I remember I am afraid, and trembling taketh hold on my flesh.

[7] Wherefore do the wicked live, become old, yea, are mighty in power?

[8] Their seed is established in their sight with them, and their offspring before their eyes.

[9] Their houses are safe from fear, neither is the rod of God upon them.

[10] Their bull gendereth, and faileth not; their cow calveth, and casteth not her calf.

[11] They send forth their little ones like a flock, and their children dance.

[12] They take the timbrel and harp, and rejoice at the sound of the organ.

[13] They spend their days in wealth, and in a moment go down to the grave.

[14] Therefore they say unto God, Depart from us; for we desire not the knowledge of thy ways.

[15] What is the Almighty, that we should serve him? and what profit should we have, if we pray unto him?

[16] Lo, their good is not in their hand: the counsel of the wicked is far from me.

[17] How oft is the candle of the wicked put out! and how oft cometh their destruction upon them! God distributeth sorrows in his anger.

[18] They are as stubble before the wind, and as chaff that the storm carrieth away.

[19] God layeth up his iniquity for his children: he rewardeth him, and he shall know it.

[20] His eyes shall see his destruction, and he shall drink of the wrath of the Almighty.

[21] For what pleasure hath he in his house after him, when the number of his months is cut off in the midst?

[22] Shall any teach God knowledge? seeing he judgeth those that are high.

[23] One dieth in his full strength, being wholly at ease and quiet.

[24] His breasts are full of milk, and his bones are moistened with marrow.

[25] And another dieth in the bitterness of his soul, and never eateth with pleasure.

[26] They shall lie down alike in the dust, and the worms shall cover them.

[27] Behold, I know your thoughts, and the devices which ye wrongfully imagine against me.

[28] For ye say, Where is the house of the prince? and where are the dwelling places of the wicked?

[29] Have ye not asked them that go by the way? and do ye not know their tokens,

[30] That the wicked is reserved to the day of destruction? they shall be brought forth to the day of wrath.

[31] Who shall declare his way to his face? and who shall repay him what he hath done?

[32] Yet shall he be brought to the grave, and shall remain in the tomb.

[33] The clods of the valley shall be sweet unto him, and every man shall draw after him, as there are innumerable before him.

[34] How then comfort ye me in vain, seeing in your answers there remaineth falsehood?

Chapter 22

[1] Then Eliphaz the Temanite answered and said,

[2] Can a man be profitable unto God, as he that is wise may be profitable unto himself?

[3] Is it any pleasure to the Almighty, that thou art righteous? or is it gain to him that thou makest thy ways perfect?

[4] Will he reprove thee for fear of thee? will he enter with thee into judgment?

[5] Is not thy wickedness great? and thine iniquities infinite?

[6] For thou hast taken a pledge from thy brother for nought, and stripped the naked of their clothing.

[7] Thou hast not given water to the weary to drink, and thou hast withholden bread from the hungry.

[8] But as for the mighty man, he had the earth; and the honourable man dwelt in it.

[9] Thou has sent widows away empty, and the arms of the fatherless have been broken.

[10] Therefore snares are round about thee, and sudden fear troubleth thee;

[11] Or darkness, that thou canst not see; and abundance of waters cover thee.

[12] Is not God in the height of heaven? and behold the height of the stars, how high they are!

[13] And thou sayest, How doth God know? can he judge through the dark cloud?

[14] Thick clouds are a covering to him, that he seeth not; and he walketh in the circuit of heaven.

[15] Hast thou marked the old way which wicked men have trodden?

[16] Which were cut down out of time, whose foundation was overflown with a flood:

[17] Which said unto God, Depart from us: and what can the Almighty do for them?

[18] Yet he filled their houses with good things: but the counsel of the wicked is far from me.

[19] The righteous see it, and are glad: and the innocent laugh them to scorn.

[20] Whereas our substance is not cut down, but the remnant of them the fire consumeth.

[21] Acquaint now thyself with him, and be at peace: thereby good shall come unto thee.

[22] Receive, I pray thee, the law from his mouth, and lay up his words in thine heart.

[23] If thou return to the Almighty, thou shalt be built up, thou shalt put away iniquity far from thy tabernacles.

[24] Then shalt thou lay up gold as dust, and the gold of Ophir as the stones of the brooks.

[25] Yea, the Almighty shall be thy defence, and thou shalt have plenty of silver.

[26] For then shalt thou have thy delight in the Almighty, and shalt lift up thy face unto God.

[27] Thou shalt make thy prayer unto him, and he shall hear thee, and thou shalt pay thy vows.

[28] Thou shalt also decree a thing, and it shall be established unto thee: and the light shall shine upon thy ways.

[29] When men are cast down, then thou shalt say, There is lifting up; and he shall save the humble person.

[30] He shall deliver the island of the innocent: and it is delivered by the pureness of thine hands.

Chapter 23

[1] Then Job answered and said,

[2] Even to day is my complaint bitter: my stroke is heavier than my groaning.

[3] Oh that I knew where I might find him! that I might come even to his seat!

[4] I would order my cause before him, and fill my mouth with arguments.

[5] I would know the words which he would answer me, and understand what he would say unto me.

[6] Will he plead against me with his great power? No; but he would put strength in me.

[7] There the righteous might dispute with him; so should I be delivered for ever from my judge.

[8] Behold, I go forward, but he is not there; and backward, but I cannot perceive him:

[9] On the left hand, where he doth work, but I cannot behold him: he hideth himself on the right hand, that I cannot see him:

[10] But he knoweth the way that I take: when he hath tried me, I shall come forth as gold.

[11] My foot hath held his steps, his way have I kept, and not declined.

[12] Neither have I gone back from the commandment of his lips; I have esteemed the words of his mouth more than my necessary food.

[13] But he is in one mind, and who can turn him? and what his soul desireth, even that he doeth.

[14] For he performeth the thing that is appointed for me: and many such things are with him.

[15] Therefore am I troubled at his presence: when I consider, I am afraid of him.

[16] For God maketh my heart soft, and the Almighty troubleth me:

[17] Because I was not cut off before the darkness, neither hath he covered the darkness from my face.

Chapter 24

[1] Why, seeing times are not hidden from the Almighty, do they that know him not see his days?

[2] Some remove the landmarks; they violently take away flocks, and feed thereof.

[3] They drive away the ass of the fatherless, they take the widow's ox for a pledge.

[4] They turn the needy out of the way: the poor of the earth hide themselves together.

[5] Behold, as wild asses in the desert, go they forth to their work; rising betimes for a prey: the wilderness yieldeth food for them and for their children.

[6] They reap every one his corn in the field: and they gather the vintage of the wicked.

[7] They cause the naked to lodge without clothing, that they have no covering in the cold.

[8] They are wet with the showers of the mountains, and embrace the rock for want of a shelter.

[9] They pluck the fatherless from the breast, and take a pledge of the poor.

[10] They cause him to go naked without clothing, and they take away the sheaf from the hungry;

[11] Which make oil within their walls, and tread their winepresses, and suffer thirst.

[12] Men groan from out of the city, and the soul of the wounded crieth out: yet God layeth not folly to them.

[13] They are of those that rebel against the light; they know not the ways thereof, nor abide in the paths thereof.

[14] The murderer rising with the light killeth the poor and needy, and in the night is as a thief.

[15] The eye also of the adulterer waiteth for the twilight, saying, No eye shall see me: and disguiseth his face.

[16] In the dark they dig through houses, which they had marked for themselves in the daytime: they know not the light.

[17] For the morning is to them even as the shadow of death: if one know them, they are in the terrors of the shadow of death.

[18] He is swift as the waters; their portion is cursed in the earth: he beholdeth not the way of the vineyards.

[19] Drought and heat consume the snow waters: so doth the grave those which have sinned.

[20] The womb shall forget him; the worm shall feed sweetly on him; he shall be no more remembered; and wickedness shall be broken as a tree.

[21] He evil entreateth the barren that beareth not: and doeth not good to the widow.

[22] He draweth also the mighty with his power: he riseth up, and no man is sure of life.

[23] Though it be given him to be in safety, whereon he resteth; yet his eyes are upon their ways.

[24] They are exalted for a little while, but are gone and brought low; they are taken out of the way as all other, and cut off as the tops of the ears of corn.

[25] And if it be not so now, who will make me a liar, and make my speech nothing worth?

Chapter 25

[1] Then answered Bildad the Shuhite, and said,

[2] Dominion and fear are with him, he maketh peace in his high places.

[3] Is there any number of his armies? and upon whom doth not his light arise?

[4] How then can man be justified with God? or how can he be clean that is born of a woman?

[5] Behold even to the moon, and it shineth not; yea, the stars are not pure in his sight.

[6] How much less man, that is a worm? and the son of man, which is a worm?

Chapter 26

[1] But Job answered and said,

[2] How hast thou helped him that is without power? how savest thou the arm that hath no strength?

[3] How hast thou counselled him that hath no wisdom? and how hast thou plentifully declared the thing as it is?

[4] To whom hast thou uttered words? and whose spirit came from thee?

[5] Dead things are formed from under the waters, and the inhabitants thereof.

[6] Hell is naked before him, and destruction hath no covering.

[7] He stretcheth out the north over the empty place, and hangeth the earth upon nothing.

[8] He bindeth up the waters in his thick clouds; and the cloud is not rent under them.

[9] He holdeth back the face of his throne, and spreadeth his cloud upon it.

[10] He hath compassed the waters with bounds, until the day and night come to an end.

[11] The pillars of heaven tremble and are astonished at his reproof.

[12] He divideth the sea with his power, and by his understanding he smiteth through the proud.

[13] By his spirit he hath garnished the heavens; his hand hath formed the crooked serpent.

[14] Lo, these are parts of his ways: but how little a portion is heard of him? but the thunder of his power who can understand?

Chapter 27

[1] Moreover Job continued his parable, and said,

[2] As God liveth, who hath taken away my judgment; and the Almighty, who hath vexed my soul;

[3] All the while my breath is in me, and the spirit of God is in my nostrils;

[4] My lips shall not speak wickedness, nor my tongue utter deceit.

[5] God forbid that I should justify you: till I die I will not remove mine integrity from me.

[6] My righteousness I hold fast, and will not let it go: my heart shall not reproach me so long as I live.

[7] Let mine enemy be as the wicked, and he that riseth up against me as the unrighteous.

[8] For what is the hope of the hypocrite, though he hath gained, when God taketh away his soul?

[9] Will God hear his cry when trouble cometh upon him?

[10] Will he delight himself in the Almighty? will he always call upon God?

[11] I will teach you by the hand of God: that which is with the Almighty will I not conceal.

[12] Behold, all ye yourselves have seen it; why then are ye thus altogether vain?

[13] This is the portion of a wicked man with God, and the heritage of oppressors, which they shall receive of the Almighty.

[14] If his children be multiplied, it is for the sword: and his offspring shall not be satisfied with bread.

[15] Those that remain of him shall be buried in death: and his widows shall not weep.

[16] Though he heap up silver as the dust, and prepare raiment as the clay;

[17] He may prepare it, but the just shall put it on, and the innocent shall divide the silver.

[18] He buildeth his house as a moth, and as a booth that the keeper maketh.

[19] The rich man shall lie down, but he shall not be gathered: he openeth his eyes, and he is not.

[20] Terrors take hold on him as waters, a tempest stealeth him away in the night.

[21] The east wind carrieth him away, and he departeth: and as a storm hurleth him out of his place.

[22] For God shall cast upon him, and not spare: he would fain flee out of his hand.

[23] Men shall clap their hands at him, and shall hiss him out of his place.

Chapter 28

[1] Surely there is a vein for the silver, and a place for gold where they refine it.

[2] Iron is taken out of the earth, and brass is molten out of the stone.

[3] He setteth an end to darkness, and searcheth out all perfection: the stones of darkness, and the shadow of death.

[4] The flood breaketh out from the inhabitant; even the waters forgotten of the foot: they are dried up, they are gone away from men.

[5] As for the earth, out of it cometh bread: and under it is turned up as it were fire.

[6] The stones of it are the place of sapphires: and it hath dust of gold.

[7] There is a path which no fowl knoweth, and which the vulture's eye hath not seen:

[8] The lion's whelps have not trodden it, nor the fierce lion passed by it.

[9] He putteth forth his hand upon the rock; he overturneth the mountains by the roots.

[10] He cutteth out rivers among the rocks; and his eye seeth every precious thing.

[11] He bindeth the floods from overflowing; and the thing that is hid bringeth he forth to light.

[12] But where shall wisdom be found? and where is the place of understanding?

[13] Man knoweth not the price thereof; neither is it found in the land of the living.

[14] The depth saith, It is not in me: and the sea saith, It is not with me.

[15] It cannot be gotten for gold, neither shall silver be weighed for the price thereof.

[16] It cannot be valued with the gold of Ophir, with the precious onyx, or the sapphire.

[17] The gold and the crystal cannot equal it: and the exchange of it shall not be for jewels of fine gold.

[18] No mention shall be made of coral, or of pearls: for the price of wisdom is above rubies.

[19] The topaz of Ethiopia shall not equal it, neither shall it be valued with pure gold.

[20] Whence then cometh wisdom? and where is the place of understanding?

[21] Seeing it is hid from the eyes of all living, and kept close from the fowls of the air.

[22] Destruction and death say, We have heard the fame thereof with our ears.

[23] God understandeth the way thereof, and he knoweth the place thereof.

[24] For he looketh to the ends of the earth, and seeth under the whole heaven;

[25] To make the weight for the winds; and he weigheth the waters by measure.

[26] When he made a decree for the rain, and a way for the lightning of the thunder:

[27] Then did he see it, and declare it; he prepared it, yea, and searched it out.

[28] And unto man he said, Behold, the fear of the Lord, that is wisdom; and to depart from evil is understanding.

Chapter 29

[1] Moreover Job continued his parable, and said,

[2] Oh that I were as in months past, as in the days when God preserved me;

[3] When his candle shined upon my head, and when by his light I walked through darkness;

[4] As I was in the days of my youth, when the secret of God was upon my tabernacle;

[5] When the Almighty was yet with me, when my children were about me;

[6] When I washed my steps with butter, and the rock poured me out rivers of oil;

[7] When I went out to the gate through the city, when I prepared my seat in the street!

[8] The young men saw me, and hid themselves: and the aged arose, and stood up.

[9] The princes refrained talking, and laid their hand on their mouth.

[10] The nobles held their peace, and their tongue cleaved to the roof of their mouth.

[11] When the ear heard me, then it blessed me; and when the eye saw me, it gave witness to me:

[12] Because I delivered the poor that cried, and the fatherless, and him that had none to help him.

[13] The blessing of him that was ready to perish came upon me: and I caused the widow's heart to sing for joy.

[14] I put on righteousness, and it clothed me: my judgment was as a robe and a diadem.

[15] I was eyes to the blind, and feet was I to the lame.

[16] I was a father to the poor: and the cause which I knew not I searched out.

[17] And I brake the jaws of the wicked, and plucked the spoil out of his teeth.

[18] Then I said, I shall die in my nest, and I shall multiply my days as the sand.

[19] My root was spread out by the waters, and the dew lay all night upon my branch.

[20] My glory was fresh in me, and my bow was renewed in my hand.

[21] Unto me men gave ear, and waited, and kept silence at my counsel.

[22] After my words they spake not again; and my speech dropped upon them.

[23] And they waited for me as for the rain; and they opened their mouth wide as for the latter rain.

[24] If I laughed on them, they believed it not; and the light of my countenance they cast not down.

[25] I chose out their way, and sat chief, and dwelt as a king in the army, as one that comforteth the mourners.

Chapter 30

[1] But now they that are younger than I have me in derision, whose fathers I would have disdained to have set with the dogs of my flock.

[2] Yea, whereto might the strength of their hands profit me, in whom old age was perished?

[3] For want and famine they were solitary; fleeing into the wilderness in former time desolate and waste.

[4] Who cut up mallows by the bushes, and juniper roots for their meat.

[5] They were driven forth from among men, (they cried after them as after a thief;)

[6] To dwell in the cliffs of the valleys, in caves of the earth, and in the rocks.

[7] Among the bushes they brayed; under the nettles they were gathered together.

[8] They were children of fools, yea, children of base men: they were viler than the earth.

[9] And now am I their song, yea, I am their byword.

[10] They abhor me, they flee far from me, and spare not to spit in my face.

[11] Because he hath loosed my cord, and afflicted me, they have also let loose the bridle before me.

[12] Upon my right hand rise the youth; they push away my feet, and they raise up against me the ways of their destruction.

[13] They mar my path, they set forward my calamity, they have no helper.

[14] They came upon me as a wide breaking in of waters: in the desolation they rolled themselves upon me.

[15] Terrors are turned upon me: they pursue my soul as the wind: and my welfare passeth away as a cloud.

[16] And now my soul is poured out upon me; the days of affliction have taken hold upon me.

[17] My bones are pierced in me in the night season: and my sinews take no rest.

[18] By the great force of my disease is my garment changed: it bindeth me about as the collar of my coat.

[19] He hath cast me into the mire, and I am become like dust and ashes.

[20] I cry unto thee, and thou dost not hear me: I stand up, and thou regardest me not.

[21] Thou art become cruel to me: with thy strong hand thou opposest thyself against me.

[22] Thou liftest me up to the wind; thou causest me to ride upon it, and dissolvest my substance.

[23] For I know that thou wilt bring me to death, and to the house appointed for all living.

[24] Howbeit he will not stretch out his hand to the grave, though they cry in his destruction.

[25] Did not I weep for him that was in trouble? was not my soul grieved for the poor?

[26] When I looked for good, then evil came unto me: and when I waited for light, there came darkness.

[27] My bowels boiled, and rested not: the days of affliction prevented me.

[28] I went mourning without the sun: I stood up, and I cried in the congregation.

[29] I am a brother to dragons, and a companion to owls.

[30] My skin is black upon me, and my bones are burned with heat.

[31] My harp also is turned to mourning, and my organ into the voice of them that weep.

Chapter 31

[1] I made a covenant with mine eyes; why then should I think upon a maid?

[2] For what portion of God is there from above? and what inheritance of the Almighty from on high?

[3] Is not destruction to the wicked? and a strange punishment to the workers of iniquity?

[4] Doth not he see my ways, and count all my steps?

[5] If I have walked with vanity, or if my foot hath hasted to deceit;

[6] Let me be weighed in an even balance, that God may know mine integrity.

[7] If my step hath turned out of the way, and mine heart walked after mine eyes, and if any blot hath cleaved to mine hands;

[8] Then let me sow, and let another eat; yea, let my offspring be rooted out.

[9] If mine heart have been deceived by a woman, or if I have laid wait at my neighbour's door;

[10] Then let my wife grind unto another, and let others bow down upon her.

[11] For this is an heinous crime; yea, it is an iniquity to be punished by the judges.

[12] For it is a fire that consumeth to destruction, and would root out all mine increase.

[13] If I did despise the cause of my manservant or of my maidservant, when they contended with me;

[14] What then shall I do when God riseth up? and when he visiteth, what shall I answer him?

[15] Did not he that made me in the womb make him? and did not one fashion us in the womb?

[16] If I have withheld the poor from their desire, or have caused the eyes of the widow to fail;

[17] Or have eaten my morsel myself alone, and the fatherless hath not eaten thereof;

[18] (For from my youth he was brought up with me, as with a father, and I have guided her from my mother's womb;)

[19] If I have seen any perish for want of clothing, or any poor without covering;

[20] If his loins have not blessed me, and if he were not warmed with the fleece of my sheep;

[21] If I have lifted up my hand against the fatherless, when I saw my help in the gate:

[22] Then let mine arm fall from my shoulder blade, and mine arm be broken from the bone.

[23] For destruction from God was a terror to me, and by reason of his highness I could not endure.

[24] If I have made gold my hope, or have said to the fine gold, Thou art my confidence;

[25] If I rejoiced because my wealth was great, and because mine hand had gotten much;

[26] If I beheld the sun when it shined, or the moon walking in brightness;

[27] And my heart hath been secretly enticed, or my mouth hath kissed my hand:

[28] This also were an iniquity to be punished by the judge: for I should have denied the God that is above.

[29] If I rejoiced at the destruction of him that hated me, or lifted up myself when evil found him:

[30] Neither have I suffered my mouth to sin by wishing a curse to his soul.

[31] If the men of my tabernacle said not, Oh that we had of his flesh! we cannot be satisfied.

[32] The stranger did not lodge in the street: but I opened my doors to the traveller.

[33] If I covered my transgressions as Adam, by hiding mine iniquity in my bosom:

[34] Did I fear a great multitude, or did the contempt of families terrify me, that I kept silence, and went not out of the door?

[35] Oh that one would hear me! behold, my desire is, that the Almighty would answer me, and that mine adversary had written a book.

[36] Surely I would take it upon my shoulder, and bind it as a crown to me.

[37] I would declare unto him the number of my steps; as a prince would I go near unto him.

[38] If my land cry against me, or that the furrows likewise thereof complain;

[39] If I have eaten the fruits thereof without money, or have caused the owners thereof to lose their life:

[40] Let thistles grow instead of wheat, and cockle instead of barley. The words of Job are ended.

Chapter 32

[1] So these three men ceased to answer Job, because he was righteous in his own eyes.

[2] Then was kindled the wrath of Elihu the son of Barachel the Buzite, of the kindred of Ram: against Job was his wrath kindled, because he justified himself rather than God.

[3] Also against his three friends was his wrath kindled, because they had found no answer, and yet had condemned Job.

[4] Now Elihu had waited till Job had spoken, because they were elder than he.

[5] When Elihu saw that there was no answer in the mouth of these three men, then his wrath was kindled.

[6] And Elihu the son of Barachel the Buzite answered and said, I am young, and ye are very old; wherefore I was afraid, and durst not shew you mine opinion.

[7] I said, Days should speak, and multitude of years should teach wisdom.

[8] But there is a spirit in man: and the inspiration of the Almighty giveth them understanding.

[9] Great men are not always wise: neither do the aged understand judgment.

[10] Therefore I said, Hearken to me; I also will shew mine opinion.

[11] Behold, I waited for your words; I gave ear to your reasons, whilst ye searched out what to say.

[12] Yea, I attended unto you, and, behold, there was none of you that convinced Job, or that answered his words:

[13] Lest ye should say, We have found out wisdom: God thrusteth him down, not man.

[14] Now he hath not directed his words against me: neither will I answer him with your speeches.

[15] They were amazed, they answered no more: they left off speaking.

[16] When I had waited, (for they spake not, but stood still, and answered no more;)

[17] I said, I will answer also my part, I also will shew mine opinion.

[18] For I am full of matter, the spirit within me constraineth me.

[19] Behold, my belly is as wine which hath no vent; it is ready to burst like new bottles.

[20] I will speak, that I may be refreshed: I will open my lips and answer.

[21] Let me not, I pray you, accept any man's person, neither let me give flattering titles unto man.

[22] For I know not to give flattering titles; in so doing my maker would soon take me away.

Chapter 33

[1] Wherefore, Job, I pray thee, hear my speeches, and hearken to all my words.

[2] Behold, now I have opened my mouth, my tongue hath spoken in my mouth.

[3] My words shall be of the uprightness of my heart: and my lips shall utter knowledge clearly.

[4] The Spirit of God hath made me, and the breath of the Almighty hath given me life.

[5] If thou canst answer me, set thy words in order before me, stand up.

[6] Behold, I am according to thy wish in God's stead: I also am formed out of the clay.

[7] Behold, my terror shall not make thee afraid, neither shall my hand be heavy upon thee.

[8] Surely thou hast spoken in mine hearing, and I have heard the voice of thy words, saying,

[9] I am clean without transgression, I am innocent; neither is there iniquity in me.

[10] Behold, he findeth occasions against me, he counteth me for his enemy,

[11] He putteth my feet in the stocks, he marketh all my paths.

[12] Behold, in this thou art not just: I will answer thee, that God is greater than man.

[13] Why dost thou strive against him? for he giveth not account of any of his matters.

[14] For God speaketh once, yea twice, yet man perceiveth it not.

[15] In a dream, in a vision of the night, when deep sleep falleth upon men, in slumberings upon the bed;

[16] Then he openeth the ears of men, and sealeth their instruction,

[17] That he may withdraw man from his purpose, and hide pride from man.

[18] He keepeth back his soul from the pit, and his life from perishing by the sword.

[19] He is chastened also with pain upon his bed, and the multitude of his bones with strong pain:

[20] So that his life abhorreth bread, and his soul dainty meat.

[21] His flesh is consumed away, that it cannot be seen; and his bones that were not seen stick out.

[22] Yea, his soul draweth near unto the grave, and his life to the destroyers.

[23] If there be a messenger with him, an interpreter, one among a thousand, to shew unto man his uprightness:

[24] Then he is gracious unto him, and saith, Deliver him from going down to the pit: I have found a ransom.

[25] His flesh shall be fresher than a child's: he shall return to the days of his youth:

[26] He shall pray unto God, and he will be favourable unto him: and he shall see his face with joy: for he will render unto man his righteousness.

[27] He looketh upon men, and if any say, I have sinned, and perverted that

which was right, and it profited me not;

[28] He will deliver his soul from going into the pit, and his life shall see the light.

[29] Lo, all these things worketh God oftentimes with man,

[30] To bring back his soul from the pit, to be enlightened with the light of the living.

[31] Mark well, O Job, hearken unto me: hold thy peace, and I will speak.

[32] If thou hast any thing to say, answer me: speak, for I desire to justify thee.

[33] If not, hearken unto me: hold thy peace, and I shall teach thee wisdom.

Chapter 34

[1] Furthermore Elihu answered and said,

[2] Hear my words, O ye wise men; and give ear unto me, ye that have knowledge.

[3] For the ear trieth words, as the mouth tasteth meat.

[4] Let us choose to us judgment: let us know among ourselves what is good.

[5] For Job hath said, I am righteous: and God hath taken away my judgment.

[6] Should I lie against my right? my wound is incurable without transgression.

[7] What man is like Job, who drinketh up scorning like water?

[8] Which goeth in company with the workers of iniquity, and walketh with wicked men.

[9] For he hath said, It profiteth a man nothing that he should delight himself with God.

[10] Therefore hearken unto me, ye men of understanding: far be it from God, that he should do wickedness; and from the Almighty, that he should commit iniquity.

[11] For the work of a man shall he render unto him, and cause every man to find according to his ways.

[12] Yea, surely God will not do wickedly, neither will the Almighty pervert judgment.

[13] Who hath given him a charge over the earth? or who hath disposed the whole world?

[14] If he set his heart upon man, if he gather unto himself his spirit and his breath;

[15] All flesh shall perish together, and man shall turn again unto dust.

[16] If now thou hast understanding, hear this: hearken to the voice of my words.

[17] Shall even he that hateth right govern? and wilt thou condemn him that is most just?

[18] Is it fit to say to a king, Thou art wicked? and to princes, Ye are ungodly?

[19] How much less to him that accepteth not the persons of princes, nor regardeth the rich more than the poor? for they all are the work of his hands.

[20] In a moment shall they die, and the people shall be troubled at midnight, and pass away: and the mighty shall be taken away without hand.

[21] For his eyes are upon the ways of man, and he seeth all his goings.

[22] There is no darkness, nor shadow of death, where the workers of iniquity may hide themselves.

[23] For he will not lay upon man more than right; that he should enter into judgment with God.

[24] He shall break in pieces mighty men without number, and set others in their stead.

[25] Therefore he knoweth their works, and he overturneth them in the night, so that they are destroyed.

[26] He striketh them as wicked men in the open sight of others;

[27] Because they turned back from him, and would not consider any of his ways:

[28] So that they cause the cry of the poor to come unto him, and he heareth the cry of the afflicted.

[29] When he giveth quietness, who then can make trouble? and when he hideth his face, who then can behold him? whether it be done against a nation, or against a man only:

[30] That the hypocrite reign not, lest the people be ensnared.

[31] Surely it is meet to be said unto God, I have borne chastisement, I will not offend any more:

[32] That which I see not teach thou me: if I have done iniquity, I will do no more.

[33] Should it be according to thy mind? he will recompense it, whether thou refuse, or whether thou choose; and not I: therefore speak what thou knowest.

[34] Let men of understanding tell me, and let a wise man hearken unto me.

[35] Job hath spoken without knowledge, and his words were without wisdom.

[36] My desire is that Job may be tried unto the end because of his answers for wicked men.

[37] For he addeth rebellion unto his sin, he clappeth his hands among us, and multiplieth his words against God.

Chapter 35

[1] Elihu spake moreover, and said,

[2] Thinkest thou this to be right, that thou saidst, My righteousness is more than God's?

[3] For thou saidst, What advantage will it be unto thee? and, What profit shall I have, if I be cleansed from my sin?

[4] I will answer thee, and thy companions with thee.

[5] Look unto the heavens, and see; and behold the clouds which are higher than thou.

[6] If thou sinnest, what doest thou against him? or if thy transgressions be multiplied, what doest thou unto him?

[7] If thou be righteous, what givest thou him? or what receiveth he of thine hand?

[8] Thy wickedness may hurt a man as thou art; and thy righteousness may profit the son of man.

[9] By reason of the multitude of oppressions they make the oppressed to cry: they cry out by reason of the arm of the mighty.

[10] But none saith, Where is God my maker, who giveth songs in the night;

[11] Who teacheth us more than the beasts of the earth, and maketh us wiser than the fowls of heaven?

[12] There they cry, but none giveth answer, because of the pride of evil men.

[13] Surely God will not hear vanity, neither will the Almighty regard it.

[14] Although thou sayest thou shalt not see him, yet judgment is before him; therefore trust thou in him.

[15] But now, because it is not so, he hath visited in his anger; yet he knoweth it not in great extremity:

[16] Therefore doth Job open his mouth in vain; he multiplieth words without knowledge.

Chapter 36

[1] Elihu also proceeded, and said,

[2] Suffer me a little, and I will shew thee that I have yet to speak on God's behalf.

[3] I will fetch my knowledge from afar, and will ascribe righteousness to my Maker.

[4] For truly my words shall not be false: he that is perfect in knowledge is with thee.

[5] Behold, God is mighty, and despiseth not any: he is mighty in strength and wisdom.

[6] He preserveth not the life of the wicked: but giveth right to the poor.

[7] He withdraweth not his eyes from the righteous: but with kings are they on the throne; yea, he doth establish them for ever, and they are exalted.

[8] And if they be bound in fetters, and be holden in cords of affliction;

[9] Then he sheweth them their work, and their transgressions that they have exceeded.

[10] He openeth also their ear to discipline, and commandeth that they return from iniquity.

[11] If they obey and serve him, they shall spend their days in prosperity, and their years in pleasures.

[12] But if they obey not, they shall perish by the sword, and they shall die without knowledge.

[13] But the hypocrites in heart heap up wrath: they cry not when he bindeth them.

[14] They die in youth, and their life is among the unclean.

[15] He delivereth the poor in his affliction, and openeth their ears in oppression.

[16] Even so would he have removed thee out of the strait into a broad place, where there is no straitness; and that which should be set on thy table should be full of fatness.

[17] But thou hast fulfilled the judgment of the wicked: judgment and justice take hold on thee.

[18] Because there is wrath, beware lest he take thee away with his stroke: then a great ransom cannot deliver thee.

[19] Will he esteem thy riches? no, not gold, nor all the forces of strength.

[20] Desire not the night, when people are cut off in their place.

[21] Take heed, regard not iniquity: for this hast thou chosen rather than affliction.

[22] Behold, God exalteth by his power: who teacheth like him?

[23] Who hath enjoined him his way? or who can say, Thou hast wrought iniquity?

[24] Remember that thou magnify his work, which men behold.

[25] Every man may see it; man may behold it afar off.

[26] Behold, God is great, and we know him not, neither can the number of his years be searched out.

[27] For he maketh small the drops of water: they pour down rain according to the vapour thereof:

[28] Which the clouds do drop and distil upon man abundantly.

[29] Also can any understand the spreadings of the clouds, or the noise of his tabernacle?

[30] Behold, he spreadeth his light upon it, and covereth the bottom of the sea.

[31] For by them judgeth he the people; he giveth meat in abundance.

[32] With clouds he covereth the light; and commandeth it not to shine by the cloud that cometh betwixt.

[33] The noise thereof sheweth concerning it, the cattle also concerning the vapour.

Chapter 37

[1] At this also my heart trembleth, and is moved out of his place.

[2] Hear attentively the noise of his voice, and the sound that goeth out of his mouth.

[3] He directeth it under the whole heaven, and his lightning unto the ends of the earth.

[4] After it a voice roareth: he thundereth with the voice of his excellency; and he will not stay them when his voice is heard.

[5] God thundereth marvellously with his voice; great things doeth he, which we cannot comprehend.

[6] For he saith to the snow, Be thou on the earth; likewise to the small rain, and to the great rain of his strength.

[7] He sealeth up the hand of every man; that all men may know his work.

[8] Then the beasts go into dens, and remain in their places.

[9] Out of the south cometh the whirlwind: and cold out of the north.

[10] By the breath of God frost is given: and the breadth of the waters is straitened.

[11] Also by watering he wearieth the thick cloud: he scattereth his bright cloud:

[12] And it is turned round about by his counsels: that they may do whatsoever he commandeth them upon the face of the world in the earth.

[13] He causeth it to come, whether for correction, or for his land, or for mercy.

[14] Hearken unto this, O Job: stand still, and consider the wondrous works of God.

[15] Dost thou know when God disposed them, and caused the light of his cloud to shine?

[16] Dost thou know the balancings of the clouds, the wondrous works of him which is perfect in knowledge?

[17] How thy garments are warm, when he quieteth the earth by the south wind?

[18] Hast thou with him spread out the sky, which is strong, and as a molten looking glass?

[19] Teach us what we shall say unto him; for we cannot order our speech by reason of darkness.

[20] Shall it be told him that I speak? if a man speak, surely he shall be swallowed up.

[21] And now men see not the bright light which is in the clouds: but the wind passeth, and cleanseth them.

[22] Fair weather cometh out of the north: with God is terrible majesty.

[23] Touching the Almighty, we cannot find him out: he is excellent in power, and in judgment, and in plenty of justice: he will not afflict.

[24] Men do therefore fear him: he respecteth not any that are wise of heart.

Chapter 38

[1] Then the LORD answered Job out of the whirlwind, and said,

[2] Who is this that darkeneth counsel by words without knowledge?

[3] Gird up now thy loins like a man; for I will demand of thee, and answer thou me.

[4] Where wast thou when I laid the foundations of the earth? declare, if thou hast understanding.

[5] Who hath laid the measures thereof, if thou knowest? or who hath stretched the line upon it?

[6] Whereupon are the foundations thereof fastened? or who laid the corner stone thereof;

[7] When the morning stars sang together, and all the sons of God shouted for joy?

[8] Or who shut up the sea with doors, when it brake forth, as if it had issued out of the womb?

[9] When I made the cloud the garment thereof, and thick darkness a swaddlingband for it,

[10] And brake up for it my decreed place, and set bars and doors,

[11] And said, Hitherto shalt thou come, but no further: and here shall thy proud waves be stayed?

[12] Hast thou commanded the morning since thy days; and caused the dayspring to know his place;

[13] That it might take hold of the ends of the earth, that the wicked might be shaken out of it?

[14] It is turned as clay to the seal; and they stand as a garment.

[15] And from the wicked their light is withholden, and the high arm shall be broken.

[16] Hast thou entered into the springs of the sea? or hast thou walked in the search of the depth?

[17] Have the gates of death been opened unto thee? or hast thou seen the doors of the shadow of death?

[18] Hast thou perceived the breadth of the earth? declare if thou knowest it all.

[19] Where is the way where light dwelleth? and as for darkness, where is the place thereof,

[20] That thou shouldest take it to the bound thereof, and that thou shouldest know the paths to the house thereof?

[21] Knowest thou it, because thou wast then born? or because the number of thy days is great?

[22] Hast thou entered into the treasures of the snow? or hast thou seen the treasures of the hail,

[23] Which I have reserved against the time of trouble, against the day of battle and war?

[24] By what way is the light parted, which scattereth the east wind upon the earth?

[25] Who hath divided a watercourse for the overflowing of waters, or a way for the lightning of thunder;

[26] To cause it to rain on the earth, where no man is; on the wilderness, wherein there is no man;

[27] To satisfy the desolate and waste ground; and to cause the bud of the tender herb to spring forth?

[28] Hath the rain a father? or who hath begotten the drops of dew?

[29] Out of whose womb came the ice? and the hoary frost of heaven, who hath gendered it?

[30] The waters are hid as with a stone, and the face of the deep is frozen.

[31] Canst thou bind the sweet influences of Pleiades, or loose the bands of Orion?

[32] Canst thou bring forth Mazzaroth in his season? or canst thou guide Arcturus with his sons?

[33] Knowest thou the ordinances of heaven? canst thou set the dominion thereof in the earth?

[34] Canst thou lift up thy voice to the clouds, that abundance of waters may cover thee?

[35] Canst thou send lightnings, that they may go, and say unto thee, Here we are?

[36] Who hath put wisdom in the inward parts? or who hath given understanding to the heart?

[37] Who can number the clouds in wisdom? or who can stay the bottles of heaven,

[38] When the dust groweth into hardness, and the clods cleave fast together?

[39] Wilt thou hunt the prey for the lion? or fill the appetite of the young lions,

[40] When they couch in their dens, and abide in the covert to lie in wait?

[41] Who provideth for the raven his food? when his young ones cry unto God, they wander for lack of meat.

Chapter 39

[1] Knowest thou the time when the wild goats of the rock bring forth? or canst thou mark when the hinds do calve?

[2] Canst thou number the months that they fulfil? or knowest thou the time when they bring forth?

[3] They bow themselves, they bring forth their young ones, they cast out their sorrows.

[4] Their young ones are in good liking, they grow up with corn; they go forth, and return not unto them.

[5] Who hath sent out the wild ass free? or who hath loosed the bands of the wild ass?

[6] Whose house I have made the wilderness, and the barren land his dwellings.

[7] He scorneth the multitude of the city, neither regardeth he the crying of the driver.

[8] The range of the mountains is his pasture, and he searcheth after every green thing.

[9] Will the unicorn be willing to serve thee, or abide by thy crib?

[10] Canst thou bind the unicorn with his band in the furrow? or will he harrow the valleys after thee?

[11] Wilt thou trust him, because his strength is great? or wilt thou leave thy labour to him?

[12] Wilt thou believe him, that he will bring home thy seed, and gather it into thy barn?

[13] Gavest thou the goodly wings unto the peacocks? or wings and feathers unto the ostrich?

[14] Which leaveth her eggs in the earth, and warmeth them in dust,

[15] And forgetteth that the foot may crush them, or that the wild beast may break them.

[16] She is hardened against her young ones, as though they were not hers: her labour is in vain without fear;

[17] Because God hath deprived her of wisdom, neither hath he imparted to her understanding.

[18] What time she lifteth up herself on high, she scorneth the horse and his rider.

[19] Hast thou given the horse strength? hast thou clothed his neck with thunder?

[20] Canst thou make him afraid as a grasshopper? the glory of his nostrils is terrible.

[21] He paweth in the valley, and rejoiceth in his strength: he goeth on to meet the armed men.

[22] He mocketh at fear, and is not affrighted; neither turneth he back from the sword.

[23] The quiver rattleth against him, the glittering spear and the shield.

[24] He swalloweth the ground with fierceness and rage: neither believeth he that it is the sound of the trumpet.

[25] He saith among the trumpets, Ha, ha; and he smelleth the battle afar off, the thunder of the captains, and the shouting.

[26] Doth the hawk fly by thy wisdom, and stretch her wings toward the south?

[27] Doth the eagle mount up at thy command, and make her nest on high?

[28] She dwelleth and abideth on the rock, upon the crag of the rock, and the strong place.

[29] From thence she seeketh the prey, and her eyes behold afar off.

[30] Her young ones also suck up blood: and where the slain are, there is she.

Chapter 40

[1] Moreover the LORD answered Job, and said,

[2] Shall he that contendeth with the Almighty instruct him? he that reproveth God, let him answer it.

[3] Then Job answered the LORD, and said,

[4] Behold, I am vile; what shall I answer thee? I will lay mine hand upon my mouth.

[5] Once have I spoken; but I will not answer: yea, twice; but I will proceed no further.

[6] Then answered the LORD unto Job out of the whirlwind, and said,

[7] Gird up thy loins now like a man: I will demand of thee, and declare thou unto me.

[8] Wilt thou also disannul my judgment? wilt thou condemn me, that thou mayest be righteous?

[9] Hast thou an arm like God? or canst thou thunder with a voice like him?

[10] Deck thyself now with majesty and excellency; and array thyself with glory and beauty.

[11] Cast abroad the rage of thy wrath: and behold every one that is proud, and abase him.

[12] Look on every one that is proud, and bring him low; and tread down the wicked in their place.

[13] Hide them in the dust together; and bind their faces in secret.

[14] Then will I also confess unto thee that thine own right hand can save thee.

[15] Behold now behemoth, which I made with thee; he eateth grass as an ox.

[16] Lo now, his strength is in his loins, and his force is in the navel of his belly.

[17] He moveth his tail like a cedar: the sinews of his stones are wrapped together.

[18] His bones are as strong pieces of brass; his bones are like bars of iron.

[19] He is the chief of the ways of God: he that made him can make his sword to approach unto him.

[20] Surely the mountains bring him forth food, where all the beasts of the field play.

[21] He lieth under the shady trees, in the covert of the reed, and fens.

[22] The shady trees cover him with their shadow; the willows of the brook compass him about.

[23] Behold, he drinketh up a river, and hasteth not: he trusteth that he can draw up Jordan into his mouth.

[24] He taketh it with his eyes: his nose pierceth through snares.

Chapter 41

[1] Canst thou draw out leviathan with an hook? or his tongue with a cord which thou lettest down?

[2] Canst thou put an hook into his nose? or bore his jaw through with a thorn?

[3] Will he make many supplications unto thee? will he speak soft words unto thee?

[4] Will he make a covenant with thee? wilt thou take him for a servant for ever?

[5] Wilt thou play with him as with a bird? or wilt thou bind him for thy maidens?

[6] Shall the companions make a banquet of him? shall they part him among the merchants?

[7] Canst thou fill his skin with barbed iron? or his head with fish spears?

[8] Lay thine hand upon him, remember the battle, do no more.

[9] Behold, the hope of him is in vain: shall not one be cast down even at the sight of him?

[10] None is so fierce that dare stir him up: who then is able to stand before me?

[11] Who hath prevented me, that I should repay him? whatsoever is under the whole heaven is mine.

[12] I will not conceal his parts, nor his power, nor his comely proportion.

[13] Who can discover the face of his garment? or who can come to him with his double bridle?

[14] Who can open the doors of his face? his teeth are terrible round about.

[15] His scales are his pride, shut up together as with a close seal.

[16] One is so near to another, that no air can come between them.

[17] They are joined one to another, they stick together, that they cannot be sundered.

[18] By his sneezings a light doth shine, and his eyes are like the eyelids of the morning.

[19] Out of his mouth go burning lamps, and sparks of fire leap out.

[20] Out of his nostrils goeth smoke, as out of a seething pot or caldron.

[21] His breath kindleth coals, and a flame goeth out of his mouth.

[22] In his neck remaineth strength, and sorrow is turned into joy before him.

[23] The flakes of his flesh are joined together: they are firm in themselves; they cannot be moved.

[24] His heart is as firm as a stone; yea, as hard as a piece of the nether millstone.

[25] When he raiseth up himself, the mighty are afraid: by reason of breakings they purify themselves.

[26] The sword of him that layeth at him cannot hold: the spear, the dart, nor the habergeon.

[27] He esteemeth iron as straw, and brass as rotten wood.

[28] The arrow cannot make him flee: slingstones are turned with him into stubble.

[29] Darts are counted as stubble: he laugheth at the shaking of a spear.

[30] Sharp stones are under him: he spreadeth sharp pointed things upon the mire.

[31] He maketh the deep to boil like a pot: he maketh the sea like a pot of ointment.

[32] He maketh a path to shine after him; one would think the deep to be hoary.

[33] Upon earth there is not his like, who is made without fear.

[34] He beholdeth all high things: he is a king over all the children of pride.

Chapter 42

[1] Then Job answered the LORD, and said,

[2] I know that thou canst do every thing, and that no thought can be withholden from thee.

[3] Who is he that hideth counsel without knowledge? therefore have I uttered that I understood not; things too wonderful for me, which I knew not.

[4] Hear, I beseech thee, and I will speak: I will demand of thee, and declare thou unto me.

[5] I have heard of thee by the hearing of the ear: but now mine eye seeth thee.

[6] Wherefore I abhor myself, and repent in dust and ashes.

[7] And it was so, that after the LORD had spoken these words unto Job, the LORD said to Eliphaz the Temanite, My wrath is kindled against thee, and against thy two friends: for ye have not spoken of me the thing that is right, as my servant Job hath.

[8] Therefore take unto you now seven bullocks and seven rams, and go to my servant Job, and offer up for yourselves a burnt offering; and my servant Job shall pray for you: for him will I accept: lest I deal with you after your folly, in that ye have not spoken of me the thing which is right, like my servant Job.

[9] So Eliphaz the Temanite and Bildad the Shuhite and Zophar the Naamathite went, and did according as the LORD commanded them: the LORD also accepted Job.

[10] And the LORD turned the captivity of Job, when he prayed for his friends: also the LORD gave Job twice as much as he had before.

[11] Then came there unto him all his brethren, and all his sisters, and all they that had been of his acquaintance before, and did eat bread with him in his house: and they bemoaned him, and comforted him over all the evil that the LORD had brought upon him: every man also gave him a piece of money, and every one an earring of gold.

[12] So the LORD blessed the latter end of Job more than his beginning: for he had fourteen thousand sheep, and six thousand camels, and a thousand yoke of oxen, and a thousand she asses.

[13] He had also seven sons and three daughters.

[14] And he called the name of the first, Jemima; and the name of the second, Kezia; and the name of the third, Keren-happuch.

[15] And in all the land were no women found so fair as the daughters of Job: and their father gave them inheritance among their brethren.

[16] After this lived Job an hundred and forty years, and saw his sons, and his sons' sons, even four generations.

[17] So Job died, being old and full of days.

NOTES